MIRACLE·MILE

IN
Los Angeles

HISTORY and ARCHITECTURE

Ruth Wallach

Charleston | London

THE
History
PRESS

Published by The History Press
Charleston, SC 29403
www.historypress.net

First published 2013

Manufactured in the United States

ISBN 978.1.60949.593.0

Library of Congress CIP data applied for.

CONTENTS

ACKNOWLEDGEMENTS

This book would not have come about without the generosity of my colleagues at the USC Libraries, particularly Giao Luong Baker, digital imaging manager, and Dace Taube, curator of the Regional History Collection. Special thanks to my family for their patience during my endless descriptions of Miracle Mile, and particularly to Andrew H. Nelson for his unconditional support of my work on this book.

Many photographs in this book were made available courtesy of the University of Southern California on behalf of the USC Libraries Special Collections. Specifically, the California Historical Society/TICOR photographic collection (CHS) was created by C.C. Pierce, a commercial photographer who documented the growth of Southern California from the late nineteenth century through the 1930s. The *Los Angeles Examiner* photograph "morgue" is a collection of images that illustrate articles in the newspaper from the 1930s through the 1950s. The "Dick" Whittington collection was created by a commercial photographer whose studio was one of the eminent photography establishments in Southern California from the mid-1920s through the 1970s. Two photographs from the Julius Shulman Archive appear courtesy of the J. Paul Getty Trust. The rest of the photographs come from the collection of the author.

INTRODUCTION

M iracle Mile, a stretch of Wilshire Boulevard, itself considered one of the grandest avenues of Los Angeles and sometimes referred to as the Grand Concourse or the Fifth Avenue of the West, is historically one of the most significant commercial real estate developments that exemplified the spread of Los Angeles westward from its classic downtown. Conceived by a land developer named A.W. (Alvah Warren) Ross in the early 1920s, it redefined "empty" tracts outside of the western boundaries of the city, where farmland was giving way to residential subdivisions, into one of the most successful commercial zones in the city. Ross's real estate ventures and legal battles with city council over zoning, which were appealed to the California Supreme Court and which he eventually won, were clearly predicated on his understanding that automobile transportation would entice commercial development out of the congested downtown and closer to the suburban neighborhoods, many of which, ironically, initially developed within reach of streetcar lines. Ross's deliberate linking of commercial development to the spread of automobile transportation was of seminal historic importance. To paraphrase Reiner Banham's influential 1971 book, *Los Angeles: The Architecture of Four Ecologies*, Miracle Mile was the first real monument to the age of the car.

Strictly speaking, the term "Miracle Mile" applies to the section of Wilshire Boulevard between Sycamore Avenue, which runs just east of La Brea Avenue, and Fairfax Avenue, which forms the district's boundary to the west. However, and not unusually for Los Angeles, where geographic terminology is not always precise, Miracle Mile connotes a larger geography. Sometimes it incorporates the section of Wilshire Boulevard stretching east of La Brea all the way to Highland Avenue. Used generically, it also includes the surrounding neighborhoods, such as the Parklabrea apartment development located to the north and the residential tracts located to the south. Miracle Mile currently encompasses several cultural institutions, among them the Los Angeles County Museum of Art (LACMA), Petersen Automotive Museum, George C. Page Museum at the La Brea Tar Pits, A+D Architecture and Design Museum and the Korean Cultural Center, as well as a variety of financial institutions. It includes a number of architecturally significant buildings, mostly built in the late 1920s and early 1930s in the Art Deco and Streamline Moderne styles. Miracle Mile also has a concentration of important mid- to high-rise commercial architecture from the 1950s to the 1980s. With waves of urban redevelopment from the late 1970s onward, Miracle Mile lost several historically important buildings that linked it to the pre–World War II economy, such as the Streamline Moderne–style Coulter's department store and the ornate Spanish Revival–style Ralphs grocery store. Recently, it also lost several mid-twentieth-century commercial buildings, the demolition of which gave way to new mixed-use apartments and condominiums.

Recognizing the historic importance of Miracle Mile's architecture and commercial planning, the Los Angeles Conservancy nominated the district for listing on the National Register of Historic Places in 1984. While it was not listed on the register, Miracle Mile is recognized as a historically important part of the architectural and economic history of Los Angeles. Today, Miracle Mile is a medium-dense commercial corridor with live/work apartment dwellings that include business establishments on the ground floor. It is beginning to resemble A.W. Ross's later vision of a Manhattan-style neighborhood with a variety of amenities available to the urban dweller within walking distance. Miracle Mile is situated within a hub of public bus and car transportation and is scheduled to be on the extension of one of the subway rail lines from downtown Los Angeles. The growth of the subway will likely further alter its architectural landscape.

Needless to say, a commercial area does not develop in a vacuum, and Miracle Mile is flanked by several residential neighborhoods dating from the late 1920s to the early 1940s. These neighborhoods, although mostly composed of single-family homes, also include fine examples of apartments built in vernacular styles fashionable in the interwar period, several of which are listed on the National Register of Historic Places. Parklabrea, an important post–World War II garden apartment complex financed by Metropolitan Life Insurance Company, is located nearby, as are several residential buildings by such notable Southern California Modernist architects as Rudolph Schindler and Gregory Ain. A residential neighborhood called Miracle Mile North, located north of Third Street, was designated by the City of Los Angeles in 1990 as a Historic Preservation Overlay Zone (HPOZ), a local designation for a historically prominent district that is relatively intact architecturally.

Miracle Mile is nearing a century since its inception, during which time its environs underwent many changes, including demographic ones. While in the 1910s and early 1920s its natural landscape was still one of undeveloped rancho lands, it was also known for a vast oil field and a commercial airport that catered to early Hollywood film stars. During the 1930s and into the post–World War II period, many Jewish families moved to this area from the eastern side of Los Angeles, something that is still evident on Fairfax Avenue and in parts of Pico Boulevard, with their many small Jewish shops, grocery stores and historic Canter's Deli. Miracle Mile is within the Fairfax District eruv, a demarcated area that allows observant Jews to carry certain items on the Sabbath without violating the biblical injunction to rest on this day.

In the 1960s and 1970s, many African American families moved to areas immediately south of Miracle Mile. Also south of Miracle Mile is a commercial hub of the Ethiopian community. After Washington, D.C., Los Angeles has the largest population of Ethiopians in the United States. Civil unrest, drought and changes in U.S. immigration law in 1965 were among the reasons for the initial Ethiopian immigration into the United States. The Refugee Act of 1980 was a catalyst for another wave of immigration, permitting many of those fleeing Mengistu Haile Mariam to settle here. The short stretch of Fairfax Avenue between Pico and Olympic Boulevards, historically a center of ethnic restaurants, became noted for Ethiopian cuisine and markets in the late 1980s. Through the efforts of the Los Angeles–based Ethiopian-American Advocacy Group, the city officially designated this stretch of Fairfax as Little Ethiopia in 2002. Miracle Mile and its vicinities are currently home to a somewhat eclectic mix of immigrant groups and ethnicities, including those of Jewish, African American, Ethiopian and Korean descent. Hebrew, Russian and Spanish can be heard in addition to English, Amharic and Korean.

Miracle Mile's late twentieth-century reemergence as an important urban hub is also marked by continuous discussions to extend the Purple subway line under Wilshire Boulevard to Fairfax Avenue and beyond from its current terminus at Western Avenue, several miles to the east. The existing network of public buses administered by the Los Angeles Metro and the Los Angeles Department of Transportation agencies is perceived for historic reasons as largely catering to a demographic composed of senior citizens and the working poor. The extension of the subway line, on the other hand, is expected to appeal to professional urbanites and to foreign, nostalgia and cultural tourists attracted by Museum Row and by the revived commercial areas around the Grove shopping mall and the historic Third Street Farmer's Market. The current interest in the history of this part of Los Angeles is predicated on several issues: the shrinking population of local elderly residents and the passing away of historic memory, changing ethnic demographics and recent efforts by the Los Angeles Conservancy in preserving Miracle Mile's historic architectural fabric.

I initially became interested in the history of Miracle Mile for purely personal reasons. As a frequent visitor to the Los Angeles County Museum of Art in the late 1980s and the mid-1990s, I was conscious of both the architectural variety on Miracle Mile and the many surface parking lots situated on what I assumed to be relatively expensive real estate. Despite the obvious fact that this stretch of Wilshire Boulevard was an old commercial area, it did not appear to attract crowds, not even on weekends, or so it seemed to me. This was true of historic places like the Carnation restaurant that was located on the eastern edge of Miracle Mile, and it was true of recent newcomers like the Georgian-Russian restaurant called Ritza, located on the south side of Wilshire Boulevard between Cochran and Dunsmuir Avenues. The latter brings back a particularly poignant memory. A friend of my father's from their days as small children in a World War II orphanage came to visit from Paris. I took him to Ritza, where Mr. Nathan, as I called him, got into a fascinating chat with one of the waiters about Georgian expatriates both knew who were still alive in Paris in the early 1990s. In return for the good memories, the waiter served us coffee and cognac gratis. Both Ritza and Carnation are long gone, and so is the Carnation building itself.

In the late 1990s, after I moved to a neighborhood that was once part of the Wilshire Vista subdivision located to the south of Miracle Mile, my daughter learned how to ride a two-wheel bicycle in the parking lot then located on the southeast corner of Hauser and Wilshire Boulevards. I knew that once there was something in this location, before it became a parking lot. This was typical of many historic sites in Los Angeles where parking surfaces replaced buildings torn down to keep up with the age of the automobile. I just did not know then that this was where the Streamline Moderne–style Coulter's

View of the "Original Berlin Wall Segments" from the collection of the Wende Museum, photographed in 2012. The segments were painted in 2009 by the artists Kent Twitchell, Farrah Karapetian, Marie Astrid González and Thierry Noir. This is part of *The Wall Project*, a public art initiative of the Wende Museum and Archive of the Cold War, Inc. *Courtesy of Ruth Wallach.*

department store once stood. This parking lot and the empty no-man's land on the southwest corner of Wilshire Boulevard and Ridgeley Drive have by now been replaced by two new apartment buildings designed in Streamline Moderne–like styles. As I write, the 1960s International Moderne–style bank building that once stood on the southeast corner of Wilshire Boulevard and La Brea Avenue is being replaced by a large commercial and residential structure that seems to be designed in a style that emulates pre–World War II Los Angeles architecture. And the massive building on the site of the 1940s Carnation Company headquarters has Art Deco–like features.

Nostalgia for the early days of Miracle Mile seems to be in vogue. However, Miracle Mile was never a static place. Certainly, A.W. Ross, the man most responsible for its existence, spent his long life trying to continuously reshape it. As the Mile enters the second decade of the twenty-first century, there are more pedestrians, more cellphones, food trucks dispensing fusion cuisines and restricted parking on the surrounding residential streets. Ten sections of the Berlin Wall, part of the Wende Museum's public art initiative that commemorates the twentieth anniversary of the reunification of Germany, are temporarily exhibited on Miracle Mile. Despite the many changes in the architecture and demographics in this part of Wilshire Boulevard, it seems to have retained a sense of place, or at least of a place name. This book will examine Miracle Mile and its environs through the history of the built environment.

Chapter 1

FROM RANCHO LAND TO REAL ESTATE BOOM

The development of the Miracle Mile section of Wilshire Boulevard from the 1920s into the early twenty-first century is part of the city's overall history of real estate speculations and of oil explorations, which date to the nineteenth century. The rise in the use of private automobile transportation in the early decades of the twentieth century also played an enormously important role. Miracle Mile was developed as a suburban shopping district, quickly spurring residential growth around it. Its origin was with Alvah Warren Ross, a realtor and land speculator whose office was located in downtown Los Angeles. The city's westernmost boundary in the late 1910s was at Western Avenue, several miles to the east of what became Miracle Mile.

A.W. Ross, as he was known through much of his professional life, came to Los Angeles from Iowa in 1893, part of a wave of that state's transplants to Southern California. Starting in 1900, he began investing in real estate, building and selling homes. Eventually, he invested in the growing suburban tracts west of the city. Together with his real estate partner, Hector N. Zahn, Ross also invested in the burgeoning oil exploration business in and around Los Angeles. As a real estate developer, Ross astutely noted that Los Angeles's growing population was increasingly dependent on automobile transportation, which reached well beyond the public rail system that has been in place since the late nineteenth century. In his book *Wilshire Boulevard: Grand Concourse of Los Angeles*, Kevin Roderick writes that already by 1920, local newspapers had mentioned that well-off and influential Angelenos preferred automobile transportation to public transit. Roderick further notes that use of local and inter-urban streetcars within the region peaked in 1924 and then began to decline, despite the fact that the population kept rapidly growing. Richard Longstreth, in his book on the economic history of Los Angeles, *City Center to Regional Mall*, writes that in 1920 the entire region had the highest ratio of cars per person in the nation.

A.W. Ross understood that the availability of cars rapidly spurred the development of dispersed suburbs, which originally grew thanks to convenient access to public transportation. He realized that as downtown became more congested, people would be willing to shop within a certain radius of where they lived and could easily get to by car. As Ross explained years later, he reasoned that this radius would be within the range of four miles. Using a map, he calculated that the best neighborhoods of the day, such as Westlake Park, Hollywood and Beverly Hills, lay within a four-mile radius, the center of which was the continuation of Wilshire Boulevard between La Brea and Fairfax Avenues. Around 1922 (sources are not terribly precise, with dates varying by a couple of years), Ross and his partners invested $54,000 into the purchase of eighteen acres of land surrounding a dirt road that would soon become the extension of Wilshire Boulevard just west of La Brea Avenue. In the early 1920s, paying $3,000 per acre in this area was considered outlandish. The venture was ridiculed as Ross's bean patch and Ross's folly.

In later years, the land that Ross so presciently purchased was described as nothing more than an expanse of rolling barley fields and grape vineyards on a desolate, wandering dirt road, with only an occasional farmhouse here and there. The corner of Wilshire Boulevard and La Brea Avenue, which had a small structure containing two storerooms, was said to be worth the price of an automobile. The next structure farther west was a two-story building on the southeast corner of Cochran Street at Wilshire Boulevard, and then there was not much else until the corner of Curson Street and Wilshire Boulevard, where a fruit market was located. Nevertheless, while some in the real estate community saw untapped commercial opportunities here, this area was not entirely as empty as Ross, his business partners and the *Los Angeles Times* later described it. In addition to some residences, there were a small airport and oil derricks on lands that belonged to the Gilmore and Hancock families, as well as an educational institution, all within the radius of approximately half a mile.

The early history of landholdings in Los Angeles is complex, with records for Spanish and Mexican land grants often incomplete and heavily contested in the early period of American California. Boundaries of landholdings were rarely precisely surveyed, contributing to the dearth of records from the pre-American period. This relative lack of legal documentation added to the speculative and litigious nature of land transactions that occurred after California became part of the United States in 1850. To add another layer of complexity, the history of changes in land ownership continued to be imprecise even after 1850. Different sources list dates for the same legal transactions that sometimes differ by a decade. Spanish names were not always recorded correctly, and the nature of business relationships between the Californio landholders and their American partners is sometimes described differently, depending on the source.

Miracle Mile is located in a small section of what was once the historic Rancho La Brea, a land grant of approximately 4,440 acres. The southerly part of the rancho encompassed today's Wilshire Boulevard near La Brea Avenue, dipping farther south to Olympic Boulevard, then following San Vicente Boulevard northwest toward Sunset Boulevard, turning northeast toward present-day Hollywood Bowl and then heading south via Gower Street toward Plymouth Boulevard. The land grant was carved out of the Rancho Rodeo de las Aguas and was given on April 8, 1828, by Jose Antonio Carillo, the mayor of the pueblo of Los Angeles, to Antonio Jose Rocha and Nemesio Dominguez. Although an entity called the Dominguez estate continued owning land around what eventually became known as Miracle Mile at least into the late 1920s, there is not a lot of information about Nemesio Dominguez himself. A lot more is known about Antonio Jose Rocha, who was born in Portugal and has been variously described as a sailor, a gunsmith and a blacksmith.

Rocha came to California in 1815 on an English trading ship, *Columbia*, and stayed on shore after the ship docked in San Pedro. Sam Clover wrote in his 1932 book, *A Pioneer Heritage*, that although Rocha deserted the ship, his application for a permit to remain in California was granted thanks to his Roman Catholic faith and the fact that, as a Portuguese, he was perceived to be ethnically close to the Spaniards. Because there was tar in the southern portion of Rancho La Brea, by terms of the grant, Angelenos could venture on rancho lands to take the brea, or tar mixed with sand, which they used to waterproof the roofs of their adobe homes. Rocha, who by that time was a prominent citizen of the pueblo, had a house that stood on the northeast corner of Spring and Court Streets that became the site of the first city hall in American Los Angeles. Rocha may have built an adobe home on the La Brea property, although it also appears that he

This undated photograph shows the courtyard of the Thompson-Gilmore adobe, which dates to the 1850s. The adobe is currently located immediately to the north of the Grove shopping mall. *Courtesy of CHS.*

never lived on the rancho. Around 1852, the Rocha family purportedly leased some of the La Brea lands to James (Don Santiago) Thompson, who served as Los Angeles county sheriff in the 1850s. It is not entirely clear whether Thompson lived in the Rocha adobe or whether he built his own. It is also possible that he built an adobe on the foundations of the Rocha house. The Thompson adobe still survives, known as the Rancho La Brea Adobe or as Gilmore Adobe. It serves as an office for the A.F. Gilmore Company and the management of the Grove shopping mall, which is located east of Fairfax Avenue on Third Street.

Antonio Jose Rocha died in 1840, and his widow, Maria Josefa Ventura, received a provisional grant to the property from the then governor Juan Bautista Alvarado. More than a decade later, the Rocha family began petitioning for a definite grant, as was required by the Land Act of 1851. This was a lengthy, litigious and expensive process. In the early 1850s, Nemesio Dominguez appears to have conveyed his portion of the rancho to Rocha's son, Jose Jorge. In 1873, the U.S. General Land Office finally issued a land patent to the Rocha family, which by this time was in financial ruin. Jose Jorge Rocha offered Henry Hancock, to whom the family owed a considerable amount of money for his survey work and legal assistance with the petition, some of the land in lieu of payment. Somewhat later, Henry Hancock, who worked as a surveyor and charted several ranchos in Southern California, and his brother John purchased much of the rest of the rancho—described as "worthless" because it was not well suited for farming—for $2.50 an acre. The Hancock brothers appear to have taken possession of the land by the 1870s, building a homestead that remained on location until it was demolished in 1950. The Hancock family owned most but not all of Rancho La Brea. In the late 1870s, the brothers also had to prove their title to the rancho in order to obtain a U.S. patent for the property. For this expensive process, they engaged Cornelius Cole, a former California senator, who presented their case in Washington, D.C. After they received official title, the Hancocks gave Cole five hundred acres of land for his services, in lieu of attorney fees. Around 1881, Cornelius Cole platted the town of Colegrove on these acres. It was located near what later

Seen here circa 1950, shortly before its demolition, is the ranch house built in the 1870s or 1880s by Henry Hancock on Rancho La Brea. In the background is the 1948 Prudential Building. *Courtesy of the* Examiner.

The Wilshire Vista neighborhood sign, a historic reference to the subdivision of the Masselin farm, photographed in 2012. *Courtesy of Ruth Wallach.*

became known as Hollywood. Both the Colegrove site and Hollywood were eventually annexed to Los Angeles in 1909.

The remaining Rancho La Brea lands did not remain intact farmland for long. In the 1870s, a French sailor named Joseph Masselin ranged sheep on the lands of Rancho La Brea and Rancho las Cienegas, adjacent to the south. Sometime in that decade, he purchased 120 acres south of what is now Wilshire Boulevard near La Brea Avenue. Masselin's farm appears to have included part of the Miracle Mile area. In 1920 and 1921, Masselin's heirs sold what remained of the ranch south of Wilshire Boulevard for residential subdivision. This became known as Wilshire Vista. Like many real estate designations in Los Angeles used to sell lots for residential development, the boundaries of the original Wilshire Vista tracts are not easy to establish. A historic sign naming the community is located on the southwest corner of Masselin Avenue and San Vicente Boulevard. The current Wilshire Vista designation extends between Hauser Boulevard to the east, Fairfax Avenue to the west, Pico Boulevard to the south and San Vicente Boulevard to the north.

When Henry Hancock died in 1883, his widow, Ida, began selling some of the land to make ends meet. In 1895, Henry Gaylord Wilshire, developer of the tony Westlake Park area just to the west of downtown Los Angeles, filed a subdivision map for a tract bearing his name that jutted into part of Rancho La Brea. The map featured a 120-foot-wide "boulevard" running westward from near downtown through the tract's center. This was the beginning of Wilshire Boulevard. As late as 1929, Wilshire Boulevard was in some parts a rutted two-lane dirt road. Its entire stretch was zoned for residential use.

James Thompson lost his portion of Rancho La Brea in a bankruptcy in 1880. Arthur Fremont Gilmore and Julius Carter, two Compton, California–based dairy farmers, acquired the Thompson adobe and the surrounding 256 acres shortly thereafter. The property's borders ran along today's La Jolla Avenue, which formed its western boundary, northward toward Rosewood Avenue and then east along Rosewood to Fairfax Avenue, where it dipped south to Beverly Boulevard, at which point it turned east toward Gardner Street and then south again toward Third Street. These boundaries encompassed much of what is today sometimes referred to as the Fairfax District and included Pan Pacific Park.

After the Gilmore-Carter partnership dissolved in 1890, Arthur Gilmore gained possession of the land and continued dairy farming. Around 1903, Gilmore struck oil while drilling for water on his farm. While his discovery prompted a boom in oil explorations on his property and on adjacent lands, drilling for oil began on Rancho La Brea considerably earlier. Shortly after her husband died, Ida Hancock, an astute, although not always successful, businesswoman in her own right, leased part of the rancho to several oil prospectors from Pennsylvania. Incorporated as the Hardison and Stewart Company, they began oil explorations on the Hancock property in 1885 with the condition that Ida Hancock and her son, George Allan, who became an influential businessman and philanthropist in Los Angeles, receive one-eighth of the oil profits and have access to the tar pools.

As Arthur Gilmore replaced his dairy cattle with oilrigs, he launched the A.F. Gilmore Company. Part of the Hancock and Gilmore properties where oil was pumped became colloquially known as the Salt Lake oil field, named after a group of oil operators from Salt Lake City who leased approximately one thousand acres for twenty years beginning in 1900. Arthur Gilmore's son, Earl Bell Gilmore, founded the Gilmore Petroleum Company. After Arthur died in 1918, Earl assumed leadership of the combined company, renamed the Gilmore Oil Company. Gilmore Oil became the largest independent oil producer on the West Coast. It operated service stations for automobiles in several locations in Los Angeles, including one on the northwest corner of Fairfax Avenue and Third Street, just north of what became Miracle Mile. What is currently known as La Brea Avenue started out as a service road for the oil wells and was used for crossing the Hancock

This aerial view from 1920 shows oil towers dotting the Hancock property northeast of what is today the intersection of Wilshire Boulevard and Fairfax Avenue, seen at the center of the photograph. The unpaved roads in the foreground became Olympic and San Vicente Boulevards. *Courtesy of CHS.*

Ranch toward Hollywood. Although most oil wells and derricks were gone from the Rancho La Brea oil fields by the late 1920s, some drilling for oil continued on the Hancock property into the 1960s. Mobil Oil took over oil production on what remained of the Salt Lake field in 1943.

While oil derricks were fast becoming part of the landscape around Wilshire Boulevard in the very early part of the twentieth century, early civil aviation also left a mark in this area. Mercury Aviation Field was located on the northwest corner of Wilshire Boulevard and Fairfax Avenue (then called Crescent Avenue). It was operated by the Mercury Aviation Company, which had several fields in and around the Los Angeles area. In 1919, Mercury Aviation moved its general offices by plane from its main field on Melrose Boulevard in Hollywood to the Wilshire field, purportedly to be close to what was fast becoming a major thoroughfare. A unique feature of the Wilshire field, a benefit of its proximity to the oil fields on the Hancock property, was its oil filling station located on the corner with Fairfax Avenue, which was equipped on one side to fill cars and on the other side to fill airplanes. Bordering the aviation field was a parking area for sightseers who often came by car to watch airplane races and other related events. The exuberance and the promise of freedom engendered in early automobile travel raised hopes that airplane travel would also become pervasive and revolutionize transportation. Mercury Aviation promoted its Wilshire field as the most complete aviation field to date and as a harbinger of safe and convenient transportation on par with, or even better than, the automobile.

In 1919, the same year that the field opened, the company announced it would begin passenger services between Los Angeles and Pasadena, Bakersfield, Fresno, Long Beach, Venice and San Francisco. Early civil aviation in the Los Angeles area attracted members of the Hollywood film community. After the movie director Cecil B. DeMille became head of the Mercury Aviation Company, the Wilshire field became known for a short period as DeMille Field No. 2 and as the DeMille-Mercury Aviation Field. In the late 1910s, Sid Chaplin, Charlie Chaplin's brother, leased the southeast corner of Wilshire and Fairfax for the Sid Chaplin Aviation Company. The first airplane load of passengers ever to be flown from New York to Los Angeles landed at the Mercury Aviation Field on Wilshire Boulevard.

In 1920, the field was taken over by Emory H. Rogers and became known as Rogers Airport, billing itself as the largest in the West. Rogers offered the City of Los Angeles free use of the field with the understanding that it would be designated as a hub to receive aerial mail and that the city would invest in building shops for visiting aviators. The real estate boom of Miracle

Early civil aviation airports were really dirt tracts, as can be seen in this 1922 photograph of Rogers Airport, which was located at Wilshire Boulevard and Fairfax Avenue. Faintly visible to the left of the billboard are two oil derricks. *Courtesy of CHS.*

Mile led by Ross and his partners quickly consigned the Rogers and Chaplin airfields to commercial redevelopment. Nevertheless, some aviation-related activities continued for a while. A very large aeronautical exhibition, the First Western Aircraft Show, was held here in November 1929 under the auspices of the Aeronautical Chamber of Commerce of America. For that purpose, an existing building on the site was enlarged into an exposition hall large enough to accommodate sixty airplanes and a variety of related equipment. Within the next decade, however, the land around the intersection of Wilshire and Fairfax was quickly redeveloped, with several important commercial structures erected.

In addition to farms, oil fields and airfields, there was a noted educational institution nearby. Within less than a mile south of Wilshire Boulevard on Cochran Avenue (then called Cahuenga Avenue), there was Page Military Academy, a noted coeducational school. Major Robert A. Gibbs and his wife, Della Page Gibbs, initially established the academy around 1906 in downtown Los Angeles. In 1908, it became a military school for boys. While the academy devoted special attention to physical culture, its mission was also to provide its students with liberal arts education, including the humanities and music. In its early days, the academy promoted itself as an institution that admitted students of all ages into a safe environment and prepared them for advanced education in the best colleges in the nation.

The Page Academy remained at various locations near downtown Los Angeles for about seven years, and around 1915, it moved to 1201 Cochran Avenue, just north of what became San Vicente Boulevard and east of today's Hauser Boulevard, which was laid out in 1924. Initially, five two-story buildings were constructed on a seven-acre plot to house dormitories, classrooms and a dining room. The structures were of brick and hollow tile faced with plaster, with arcades opening to a central courtyard area. The headquarters of the school were in the Gibbses' own home on Cochran Avenue. According to the *Los Angeles Times*, the academy promoted itself as "a place where young boys could be educated without the menace and overlordship of high-school cadets" and became known as the "big school for little boys." According to Major Gibbs's own account in 1932, "In those days we were out in the country…Only a few scattered ranch-houses were in sight. Even the Los Angeles High School had not been erected."

The school also offered such extracurricular activities as singing in the glee club, playing in the band and taking part in theatrics. A dozen years after the Page Academy moved to Cochran Avenue, it boasted enrollment of over 250 students. Additional buildings were constructed over time. In the 1930s, the school proudly publicized its international student body, with some students coming from such geographically far-flung places as Chile, Bolivia, Venezuela, England and South Africa. In 1941, Page purchased the Oneonta Military Academy, which was located in Culver City several miles to the west. The Oneonta school, formerly known as the Pacific Military School, was established by Harry Culver, Culver City's developer. Culver also mediated the $250,000 transaction with the Page Academy. The Culver City–based Page-Oneonta Academy's mission was to educate high school cadets, while the Page Military Academy on Cochran Avenue remained a place for educating younger boys. The school stayed at this location until 1958, by which time it was surrounded by single-family houses. A large apartment complex was built in 1963 on the northwest corner of San Vicente Boulevard and Cochran Avenue, where several of the academy's buildings once stood. Page Academy grew into a network of schools, and the Gibbs family and their descendants continued playing an important role in the Southern California business and educational communities into the post–World War II period.

Page Military Academy is shown in this 1925 photograph. It was located on the northwest corner of San Vicente Boulevard and Cochran Avenue. *Courtesy of the* Examiner.

It is true that the southwest portion of Rancho La Brea and the nearby lands of Rancho las Cienegas were indeed out in the country, as later boosters of westward expansion of Los Angeles proclaimed. However, they were not merely empty. Oil production, the airfield and the Page Academy attracted considerable human activity. There were also paleontological excavations conducted on the Hancock family lands, spurred by George Allan Hancock's own scientific interests, that were yielding considerable amounts of prehistoric bones and attracted local tourists. Nevertheless, already by the late nineteenth century, the powerful Los Angeles real estate industry saw the ranchos as ripe for urban development.

By the early 1910s, the western boundary of Los Angeles lay near Western Avenue, a north–south artery. Wilshire Boulevard within city limits was zoned for residential use. As land farther west of Western was annexed to the city, the extension of Wilshire Boulevard was also zoned for residential use. The Wilshire Improvement Association, composed of property owners along Wilshire, which was sometimes hyped as the Fifth Avenue of the West, was formed circa 1910 to lobby the city's realty board for street improvements and for commercial development. By 1920, according to Marc Weiss's book *The Rise of the Community Builders*, the Realty Board, with the support of the chamber of commerce and the city planning commission, formed a committee to develop a zoning plan for the city's westward expansion. Shortly thereafter, a rift developed among members of the realty board. Some dealers in properties located along Wilshire Boulevard saw potential in developing it as an office and retail street for the affluent residents of the western suburban enclaves near Los Angeles who no longer wanted to travel for business and commerce all the way to a downtown that was rapidly becoming congested. Others on the board, which was dominated by downtown brokers and large-scale residential subdividers, wanted to extend residential zoning westward. Shaping the future growth of Los Angeles was no trivial matter. According to Weiss, during the speculative land boom that lasted from 1922 to 1924, nearly four thousand subdivisions were staked out beyond the borders of the city and opened for sale.

A.W. Ross, who wanted to develop his holdings into a commercial center, was among those developers who fought with city council over the zoning ordinance. After the city denied Ross and his partner, Hector Zahn, the permit to erect a business structure on Wilshire Boulevard between Cochran and Dunsmuir Streets, the two filed a petition with the appellate court. Eventually, they took their case to the state Supreme Court, arguing that removing restrictions on commercial development would considerably increase the value of the lots along Wilshire Boulevard. At the same time, Ross and Zahn also sought relief from the setback ordinance, which required that all buildings on Wilshire Boulevard be set back a minimum of fifteen feet from the street line. Their argument was probably made in preparation for providing parking lots behind the proposed business establishments.

Ross wielded considerable influence with city council, through which he was able to exclude competitors from the initial development of Miracle Mile. He pressured the council to change zoning for the individual lots that he purchased at residential zoning prices so that he could then attempt to sell or lease them to his partners for about $100 for each frontage foot of commercial development. Wilshire Boulevard was eventually rezoned through such spot zoning to allow for construction of commercial buildings on a lot-by-lot basis. Ross—whose realty, by some accounts, was located in a small house on the south corner of Wilshire Boulevard and Ogden Drive; by other accounts, somewhat east at the intersection of Wilshire and Curson Avenue; and by yet other accounts, just west of Hauser Boulevard—initially named his holdings the Wilshire Boulevard Center. A friendly investor is supposed to have remarked that the way Ross talked about his real estate venture, one would think this was really a miracle mile. Ross appropriated this term, which seems to have come into official use by 1928 to name the section of Wilshire Boulevard between Sycamore Street and Fairfax Avenue.

Ross, by all accounts, was an extremely astute real estate developer who paid considerable attention to the manner in which Los Angeles was growing. He exerted tremendous influence on the way Miracle Mile grew and changed into the second half of the twentieth century. Thanks to the explosive growth in the use of the automobile as a means of transportation, the city quickly became suburbanized. Already in his classic study, *Southern California Country: An Island on the Land*, published in 1946, Carey McWilliams had observed that one of the distinguishing aspects of Los Angeles was its lower urban density relative to other American urban centers and higher suburban density relative to other suburbs in the country. This was partly a result of rail- and, later, car-oriented growth of single-family housing tracts. Even before World War II, in order to serve the ever-expanding residential neighborhoods, new retail zones emerged as linear strips along the major boulevards, with branches of stores sometimes surpassing their downtown headquarters in popularity.

By the late 1920s, Miracle Mile had begun to shape into an attractive shopping district. Getting the fashionable men's clothing retailer Desmond's, located in downtown Los Angeles, to open a branch at the Wilshire Tower building in 1929 was a big coup for A.W. Ross and his partners, who used it to attract other retailers. The Miracle Mile Desmond's immediately attracted attention. As Richard Longstreth explains in *City Center to Regional Mall*, the enormous neon sign bearing the firm's name on top of the tower gave Desmond's a singular presence that was unrivaled for a long time. Desmond's was quickly followed by other clothing retailers, such as Silverwood's, Myer Siegel, C.H. Baker and others, which saw an opportunity to capitalize on the economic power of shoppers living west of downtown. By the late 1920s and early 1930s, Miracle Mile also had a Ralphs grocery store, some drugstores and a few restaurants.

In order to woo the car-driving shopper, Miracle Mile retail establishments had two major entries, one from the Wilshire sidewalk for pedestrian shoppers and one from the ample (by the standards of the time) parking lots, most of which were situated in the back. The architectural idiom of Miracle Mile at that time was a mix of low-rise and height-limit Spanish Colonial Revival, Art Deco and Streamline Moderne commercial structures. Exterior design included flashy elements to attract both pedestrians and car-driving customers. Some, like the E. Clem Wilson Building, constructed in 1930 on the northeast corner of Wilshire Boulevard and La Brea Avenue, had imposing towers that could bear large signs. Others, like the 1929 bank building located just east of the Wilson tower on Wilshire Boulevard, had sumptuous exterior detail.

Above: Ralphs supermarket, housed in a Spanish Revival–style structure designed in 1928 by Stiles O. Clements, is seen to the left in this 1940s photograph. Coulter's, designed by Clements in 1938, is located to the right. In the distance are the Wilshire Tower, Dominguez and E. Clem Wilson buildings. *Courtesy of "Dick" Whittington.*

Right: The E. Clem Wilson Building is photographed from the southwest corner of Wilshire Boulevard and La Brea Avenue, circa 1930. Known for a long time as the Mutual of Omaha Building, it is now known as the Samsung building because of the company's logo on the top of the tower. *Courtesy of the* Examiner.

Left: The Deco Building, located just east of the E. Clem Wilson tower, was designed in 1929 by Morgan, Walls & Clements for Security National Bank. Photographed in 1930. *Courtesy of the* Examiner.

Below: The Darkroom, an example of a programmatic architectural façade, was designed by Marcus P. Miller in 1937 for a photography shop. Photographed in 2011. *Courtesy of Ruth Wallach.*

A somewhat later example, the Darkroom, located in a commercial block initially built in stages in the late 1920s and early 1930s, had a storefront designed in 1937 by Marcus P. Miller to look like a camera. Residential areas comprising single-family homes and small apartment buildings began to quickly develop to the south and north of the commercial mile. After World War II, notable architects, such as Charles Luckman, Sidney Eisenshtat and Welton Becket, designed commercial buildings in the International Modern architectural style.

Until he died in 1967, A.W. Ross was deeply involved and influential in the Miracle Mile business community, constantly

A.W. Ross was immortalized in this 1956 bronze bust by Holger and Helen Jensen. Photographed in 2010. *Courtesy of Ruth Wallach.*

advocating further and denser development of this area. While he did not succeed in realizing many of his schemes, he certainly left an indelible mark on the urban landscape of Los Angeles. One of the presumed sites of Ross's office, the northeast corner of Wilshire Boulevard and Curson Avenue, is commemorated by a bronze bust made in 1956 by the sculptors Holger and Helen Jensen. The bust was dedicated in this public location during a ceremony attended by the mayor of Los Angeles in 1964. The inscription on the dedication plaque on the base of the bust reads: "A.W. Ross, founder and developer of the Miracle Mile. Vision to see, wisdom to know, courage to do." The first sentence came from advertisements for Ross's realty, which appeared in 1930s newspapers to promote and further the economic development of Miracle Mile. The second sentence is a reference to Ross's tireless perseverance, despite the early ridicule of his unrealized real estate investment, and to his dream to see Miracle Mile encompass the entire Wilshire Boulevard from Grand Avenue in downtown Los Angeles to the ocean in Santa Monica.

Chapter 2

THE URBAN LANDSCAPE OF THE EXPANDING CITY

The Miracle Mile section of Wilshire Boulevard, originally designated by its principal developer, A.W. Ross, as stretching from Sycamore Avenue to Fairfax Avenue, was characteristic of the relentless growth of Los Angeles that began in the 1880s. The city's and the region's quick growths were in part the consequence of the influx of winter tourists from other parts of the United States, many of whom stayed permanently thanks to Southern California's mild climate. Other contributors to the city's expansion included the availability of relatively cheap land, much of it from former Mexican ranchos; accessibility to rail transportation; and the discovery of oil. While Los Angeles grew in all directions, its westward move corresponded to the laying out of residential tracts that were intended to attract members of the professional and upper socioeconomic classes. They had race-based covenants, as well as architectural restrictions.

Although downtown Los Angeles continued to be the center of government and commerce, and Broadway Boulevard remained a major shopping hub into the twenty-first century—albeit catering to a variety of socioeconomic and ethnic populations—the city was rapidly suburbanizing. The westward development of upscale single-family residential neighborhoods was predicated on their eventual and swift incorporation into city limits. In the 1910s and early 1920s, several noted residential subdivisions were laid out on the eastern edges of Rancho La Brea and on other former rancho lands abutting Wilshire Boulevard. Wilshire was originally planned by Henry Gaylord Wilshire and others as a residential avenue bordered by grand mansions surrounded by park-like landscaping. Its rapid growth was undoubtedly influential in contributing to A. W. Ross's vision for a business and shopping center that he originally called Wilshire Boulevard Center and later renamed Miracle Mile. Many of the homes in the new western subdivisions around Wilshire Boulevard, such as Windsor Square, were designed by successful Los Angeles–based architects and builders in historic revival styles such as Spanish Colonial, Tudor or Mediterranean—and in some of the earlier subdivisions, such as Wilshire Park, in Craftsman Bungalow style—all set on landscaped lots. Because some of these subdivisions have retained their historic architectural characteristics, several of them have been designated by the City of Los Angeles as Historic Preservation Overlay Zones (HPOZs), a local name for historically significant neighborhoods.

THE RESIDENTIAL CONTEXT FOR THE FOUNDING OF MIRACLE MILE

Early twentieth-century residential real estate ventures provided an important context for the establishment of Miracle Mile. In the 1910s, Los Angeles's western boundary along Wilshire Boulevard extended just west of Western Avenue, with lands beyond belonging to the Hancock and Rimpau families and to the heirs of various mid-nineteenth-century homesteaders. In the 1880s and 1890s, groups of Los Angeles businessmen set their sights on some of the rancho tracts in anticipation of the city's expansion and of potential financial profit. Nevertheless, several decades passed before some of these plans were realized. One of the earliest was the neighborhood currently known as Wilshire Park, which was annexed to the city in 1909. It came under development by the firms of Robert McGarvin & Marcus Bronson and the David Barry Company somewhat earlier, around 1905, on portions of land that were once part of Rancho Las Cienegas. The neighborhood, located just south of Wilshire Boulevard extending to Olympic Boulevard, bordered by Wilton Place to the east and Bronson Avenue to the west, was marketed as being on high ground, with the advantage of "large lots and wide streets, with carefully-considered building restrictions" and views of the city.

In 1911, following the success of Wilshire Park, one of the largest residential real estate deals to date, which encompassed 200 acres located on the extreme western end of what was called Wilshire District, was announced. The term "Wilshire District" appears to have been applied to whatever lay beyond the city's western boundary along Wilshire Boulevard until La Brea Avenue. The 200 acres were purchased from their holder, Windsor Square Land Company, by the newly incorporated Windsor Square Investment Company. According to the *Los Angeles Times*, several noted businessmen and financiers, among them Maurice S. Hellman and Herman Boettcher, purchased the land in 1885 from the estate of John C. Plummer, a Canadian immigrant who settled in Los Angeles in the late 1860s and was granted 640 acres west of the city for a homestead. The Plummer lands lay between Wilshire Boulevard and Temple Street (now Beverly Boulevard) to the north, bordered by Western Avenue to the east and Rancho La Brea to the west.

Hellman and his partners filed the articles of incorporation for the Windsor Square Land Company in 1892. The Windsor Square Investment Company syndicate was incorporated shortly before the 1911 purchase of the two hundred acres, which by this time lay within city limits. The syndicate included noted businessmen, among them members of the Hellman family and Robert A. Rowan, an important real estate agent in Los Angeles, who surveyed and recorded this land for subdivision. It became known as Windsor Square and was hailed as the most exclusive residential neighborhood in the Los Angeles area, rivaling Chester Place located north of the University of Southern California. According to the plans, the lots were to be at least one hundred feet at the frontage and three hundred feet in depth. The overall park-like design specified homes costing between $10,000 and $30,000 at a time when a modest family bungalow could be purchased for several thousand dollars.

Although automobile ownership was beginning to alter transportation in the city, Windsor Square was still advertised as being served by the Melrose Avenue electric car line and by the planned extension of the Temple Boulevard streetcar line. Landscaping for this residential development was designed by Paul J. Howard, a noted horticulturalist and owner of an extensive nursery business. Incidentally, in 1923, Howard opened one of his nurseries on a five-acre site on La Brea Avenue at Third Street, in the Miracle Mile area. Today, historic Windsor Square, which expanded farther northward after World War I, lies between Wilshire Boulevard to the south and Beverly Boulevard to the north. Its eastern boundary is Van Ness Avenue, and it is bounded to the west by Arden Boulevard. Most of Windsor Square's Wilshire Boulevard frontage was rezoned in the twentieth century for commercial use. Windsor Square was designed HPOZ in 2004.

In 1920–21, the Tracy E. Shoults Company and its associate, the builder Sidney H. Woodruff, invested in the extension of Windsor Square toward the north, which they called New Windsor Square. This was part of Shoults's and Woodruff's larger investment into developing several residential tracts to the north and northwest of Windsor Square, which resulted in another noted neighborhood, Windsor Heights, also subdivided by Robert A. Rowan & Company. Windsor Heights was heavily promoted because of its closeness to the prestigious Marlborough School for girls and to the grounds of the Wilshire Country Club, laid out in 1919. This and other residential subdivisions nearby were also said to be among the finest residential districts in Los Angeles.

In order to boost the public's interest in the districts, Woodruff and his Western Construction Company built a demonstration house in the adobe style at 201 Larchmont Boulevard on the southwest corner with Second Street. Constructed under the direction of a man named Juan Fernandez, said to have extensive practical experience with adobe construction in Spain and Mexico, it was promoted as the grandest adobe structure erected in California since the middle of the nineteenth century. The house was opened to public viewing in January 1921 and became known as the Adobe Electrical Home. Woodruff said it was an experiment to showcase modern household conveniences. He touted the house for its practical and artistic design and as an example of good architecture adapted to the climate of Southern California. The names of all the builders, contractors and suppliers for the house were printed in the *Los Angeles Times*. Forty-eight thousand people came to see it, marveling at the modern electrical devices, which included a warmer just for baby milk. The house itself cost about $35,000 to construct, with electrical installations, appliances and two automobiles in the garage amounting to an additional $20,000 and furniture and items of interior décor representing an extra $30,000.

In March 1922, the developer Tracy E. Shoults purchased the completely furnished house, where he resided until his death in 1923. The Adobe Electric Home, no longer extant, was one of the many demonstration homes built in cooperation between developers and construction firms in Los Angeles into the middle of the twentieth century. They were open to the public and promoted by developers and newspapers as homes of the future. Some of them were later constructed on Wilshire Boulevard at or near Miracle Mile.

In 1919, George Allan Hancock leased some of the oil fields of his Rancho La Brea Oil Company to the Wilshire Country Club, located west of Windsor Square and of the neighborhoods that grew around it. The country club became the center of an exclusive residential neighborhood called Hancock Park. George Allan Hancock specified that the residences be set fifty feet into the lots away from street frontage, similar to the park-like settings of the other exclusive subdivisions along Wilshire Boulevard. While a large portion of Hancock Park was developed in the 1920s and 1930s, the smaller lots closer to Melrose Boulevard, its northern boundary, were developed after World War II. Hancock Park is located between Wilshire Boulevard to the south, Rossmore Avenue to the east, Melrose Boulevard to the north and Highland Avenue to the west. It was designated HPOZ in 2006.

Another exclusive residential development that grew along Wilshire Boulevard, on its south side, was Fremont Place. A partnership consisting of the Charles B. Ingram Company, George H. Briggs and the David Barry Company held land west of Crenshaw Boulevard since 1908, laying ground for a fashionable park-like, forty-seven-acre subdivision zoned for single-family residences. The original forty-eight lots measured two hundred by two hundred feet, with homes planned at the cost of at least $7,500. The first mansion, designed by the noted Los Angeles architect John C. Austin, was built in 1916. For most passersby, even today, Fremont Place is primarily noted for its elaborate Greek Revival–style gateways located at the north and south entrances to this gated neighborhood. The gateways were designed by J. Martyn Haenke for the intersections of what were then known as Easterly and Westerly Drives (now Fremont Place West and Fremont Place) with Wilshire Boulevard and at the intersection of the same streets with Country Club Drive (now Olympic Boulevard). Each gateway was designed to be seventy-six feet wide and eighteen feet high, framed by granite columns, costing $12,000. The actual columns were built of cast concrete and, according to Kevin Roderick, delineated Fremont Place as a special and exclusive neighborhood for the weekend pleasure tourists.

By 1960, many of the original lots in Fremont Place had been further subdivided, and the neighborhood had seventy-three residences located between Wilshire Boulevard to the north, Olympic Boulevard to the south, Lucerne Boulevard to the east and Muirfield Road to the west. Lots along Wilshire Boulevard were eventually sold for commercial development.

In 1921, the David Barry Company also began to subdivide the Wilshire Crest tract, just west of Fremont Place. Like Fremont Place, Wilshire Crest was located south of Wilshire Boulevard on the former Rancho las Cienegas, which by then belonged to the Rimpau family. In 1920, riding the wave of the city's relentless development westward, the Rimpau brothers engaged

The gateways of Fremont Place were designed to set off the exclusivity of this neighborhood, located just south of Wilshire Boulevard and west of Crenshaw Avenue. Shown in this 2012 photograph is one of the gateway columns. *Courtesy Ruth of Wallach.*

the services of the civil engineer George W. Tuttle and Paul J. Howard, the horticulturalist who was also working on the landscaping of Windsor Square, to oversee the subdivision of the property into 321 residential lots. Three streets running parallel to Wilshire Boulevard to the south and five streets crossing it were laid out. Howard planned Italian-style sunken gardens with stone stairways, balustrades and bridges for twenty-five of the largest lots. A recreational area for children was also planned. The *Los Angeles Times* declared it an ideal subdivision because it occupied the highest ground of Wilshire Boulevard west of Western Avenue, above the exclusive Fremont Place and Windsor Square subdivisions to its east. Wilshire Crest was also publicized as commanding panoramic views of the city and of the mountains to the north.

As was the case with the other new residential developments along Wilshire Boulevard, Wilshire Crest was promoted as an exclusive neighborhood. A fifty-year protection prohibited businesses and apartments from being erected. In addition, a building restriction prohibited construction of any private residences costing less than $10,000. Home sites were deemed large enough to accommodate such amenities as tennis courts, swimming pools or teahouses. In 1922, the *Los Angeles Times*, for decades a promoter of private real estate interests in the city and surrounding areas, announced that it would award several pieces of property and twenty automobiles as prizes to candidates who would generate the most subscriptions to the newspaper. Among the prizes was a new home valued at $16,500 in Wilshire Crest, designed in the Mediterranean style by Mendel Meyer and Phillip Holler and financed by the *Times*. The property included landscaping, also designed by Meyer and Holler and laid out by the Beverly Hills Nursery. The *Times*'s promotion of its prize house was educational, and its articles explained to the general public the symbiotic interaction between its architecture and the landscape.

The two-story house, constructed by the Milwaukee Building Company, was located on Tremaine Avenue between Eighth and Ninth Streets, overlooking the Arroyo de los Jardines, or Creek of the Gardens, which originated in the Hollywood Hills and flowed into Ballona Creek through the Wilshire Country Club and through Wilshire Crest near the intersection of Olympic Boulevard and Longwood Avenue. Its sloping banks were landscaped and adorned with several picturesque concrete bridges. Tremaine Avenue was called the most beautiful street in the entire Wilshire District, as the general area between Crenshaw and La Brea Avenues was called. It was planted with *Sterculia* and *Acacia latifolia*, both trees featured on the grounds of the 1915 San Diego Exposition, which was extremely influential in the architectural and horticultural landscape of Southern California. The *Times* published quite a few articles publicizing its prize house and included a long list of the builders and contractors who worked on it. Local tourists traveling in motorcars and potential buyers were instructed to take Wilshire Boulevard to the "high ground just west of Fremont Place and Windsor

Square." The neighborhood was said to be close to the recently constructed Los Angeles High School, the Marlborough School for girls and two private military schools, as well as to the Eleventh Street yellow car line.

The winners of the *Times*-sponsored Wilshire Crest house, a couple identified as Mr. and Mrs. M.L. Hazzard of Monrovia, were announced on September 10, 1922. Whether Mr. Hazzard was the banker M.L. Hazzard, known for his financial investment in Imperial Valley was not noted by the *Times*. Nor did the newspaper follow up on what happened to the house once the Hazzards took possession of it. Such publicity by the *Times* raised the popularity of Wilshire Boulevard developments. Much of the historic Wilshire Crest is currently known as Brookside, with borders comprising Wilshire Boulevard to the north, Muirfield Avenue to the east, Olympic Boulevard to the south and Highland Avenue to the west.

The neighborhoods described here were exclusively single-family residential, and this was true for the entire stretch of Wilshire Boulevard between Crenshaw and Highland Avenues. Nonresidential developments were few and far between. Downtown Los Angeles was still the main commercial hub. Nevertheless, Larchmont Village, located to the north of Windsor Square and Hancock Park and patterned after a New York City suburb, had a commercial main street. And in the 1920s, several notable institutions developed in these environs, although most were not commercial in nature. The Wilshire United Methodist Church, located at 4350 Wilshire Boulevard, on the southwest corner with Plymouth Boulevard, was designed in a mixture of Romanesque and Gothic architectural styles by the architecture firm Allison and Allison and dedicated in 1924. The church was designated Los Angeles Historic Cultural Monument #114 in 1973. Several other churches to serve parishioners in the new neighborhoods were built over time in the 1920s and 1930s, as well as some cultural and educational institutions.

Located just to the west of the Wilshire United Methodist Church, at 4400 Wilshire Boulevard, southwest of the intersection with Lucerne Boulevard, is the Wilshire Ebell Theater and Club. The club building, constructed in 1927, was designed by the architects Sumner P. Hunt and Silas R. Burns in the Beaux-Arts style. A particularly notable and visible feature of the building is the entrance framed in an elegant arch capped by a cartouche bearing the letter *E*. Above it is a balustrade that holds two urns. The Ebell itself was founded in 1894 as a women's educational and philanthropic organization and is one of America's oldest and largest women's clubs. In 1982, the building was designated Los Angeles Historic Cultural Monument #250 and has been on the National Register of Historic Places since 1994.

View of the Georgian Revival–style Los Angeles High School, built in 1917 on the southeast corner of Olympic Boulevard and Rimpau Avenue. Photographed in 1960. *Courtesy of the* Examiner.

The Marlborough School, the oldest independent girls' school in Southern California, opened at its current location on Rossmore Avenue, just north of Third Street, in 1916. At that time, the Marlborough School was said to be on the western edge of Windsor Square within walking distance of the Melrose Avenue car line. The preliminary designs for the American Colonial Revival–style campus were drawn by the architect John C. Austin. Farther to the west, adjacent to Wilshire Boulevard, is the John Burroughs Middle School, located on McCadden Place. Designed by architects employed by the school board in a Georgian Revival architectural style, it opened in 1924.

In 1917, the Los Angeles High School relocated from downtown to its current location at 4600 Olympic Boulevard, on the southeast corner with Rimpau Boulevard and immediately to the south of the Wilshire residential neighborhoods. Originally designed in Georgian Revival style, the school was considerably damaged during the 1971 earthquake. The current campus

View of the bench designed by Brent Spears, titled *Literary Mosaic*, that is located near the Memorial branch library. Photographed in 2009. *Courtesy of Ruth Wallach.*

was designed by Al Whittle Associates and Kennard, Delahousie & Gault and opened in 1977. To honor classmates who had fallen in World War I, students purchased a plot of land opposite the school on the north side of Olympic Boulevard for a memorial park. The Memorial branch library of the city's public library system opened in the park in 1930. Designed in a Gothic Revival style by the architect John C. Austin, its windows incorporate stained glass by Judson Studios. The library building was designated Los Angeles Historic Cultural Monument # 81 in 1971 and was listed in 1987 on the National Register of Historic Places. In 2008, a mosaic bench by Brent Spears, titled *Literary Mosaic*, was installed in the park. Farther to the west, Wilshire Crest Elementary School opened in 1923 on the northeast corner of Country Club Drive (now Olympic Boulevard) and Orange Drive. The preliminary plans for it were drawn by the architect Otto H. Neher.

Among the early commercial structures built in this part of the Wilshire District is the Farmers Insurance building, located at 4680 Wilshire Boulevard. In 1935, Farmers' Automobile Inter-Insurance Exchange purchased a large parcel of land on the southeast corner of Wilshire and Rimpau Boulevards, which extended south to Eighth Street. Groundbreaking for the building took place in 1937. The original three-story office building was designed in a combination of Moderne and Art Deco styles by Albert R. Walker and Percy A. Eisen, with Claud Beelman as consulting architect. In 1949, the building rose to seven stories, with the seamless expansion designed by John Fortune and Associates. In 1965, at a time when portions of Wilshire Boulevard's commercial areas were experiencing uncertain economic times, the city board of zoning appeals granted a zoning variance to Farmers Underwriters Association to build a plant for its electronic data processing division on the Rimpau Boulevard side. The board's decision was supported by the mayor's Economic Development Board, which warned that if the city did not encourage and support commercial zoning, many businesses would move to other counties. A three-story annex in the Modernist style, designed by the architecture firm of Stiles and Robert Clements, was built in 1984 somewhat west of the original building on the corner of Wilshire Boulevard with Keniston Avenue.

In 1922, the developers Walter G. McCarty and John A. Vaughan offered what they called the last tracts on Wilshire Boulevard in the bon-ton part of Los Angeles that were available for subdivision. This allusion to gentility made for a good advertising campaign. McCarty and Vaughan called the 85 acres Wilshire Vista. They bought the property from the heirs of Joseph Masselin, a French-born rancher who purchased 120 acres of land west of Los Angeles in 1870. In the nineteenth century, the city was growing toward the east; thus, its western portions were less desirable and, therefore, cheaper. The boundaries of Wilshire Vista were rather fuzzy, but the realtors advertised it as being located between Pico Boulevard to the south and Wilshire Boulevard to the north, centered on Cahuenga Avenue (soon renamed to Cochran), where the McCarty and Vaughan realty offices were located. Wilshire Vista was advertised as being on the route of a newly planned Pacific Electric car line that was supposed to run on San Vicente Boulevard, which cut diagonally across the subdivision, within a few minutes' walk to the Page Academy. The lots in the subdivision were smaller than on the famous Wilshire Boulevard–fronting residential tracts to the east, and the houses, quite a few of which were built in Spanish and Tudor Revival styles, were more modest. Many of these houses were constructed and sold in the mid- to late 1920s by the realty firms Commercial Construction Company and by the John A. Evans Corporation.

Another residential development along Wilshire Boulevard that contextualized Miracle Mile's eventual success was Carthay Center, located on the border with Beverly Hills. The neighborhood is known to many Angelenos primarily from the photographs of the historic movie theater that is no longer extant. Carthay Center was planned by J. Harvey McCarthy on 136 acres of land that his consortium, called the Carthay Center Holding Corporation, purchased in 1922 from Samuel K. Rindge and the Sherman Company. McCarthy envisioned Carthay Center as a modern community of upper-middle-class residences. Within several months of the purchase, McCarthy formally opened the tracts for public bidding. The initial plans for the subdivision were drawn by the landscape architects W. David Cook and George Hall in association with consulting architects Aleck Curlett and Claud Beelman. In order to attract investors and buyers, McCarthy also announced that the Carthay Center Holding Corporation would considerably improve the lots. These improvements included laying out wide paved streets and parkways and the installation of ornamental streetlights. Carthay Center was the first neighborhood in the city to have its utilities buried under the streets, a fact that was publicized at that time as advanced urban planning. Bisecting the subdivision from Wilshire Boulevard to the north and Country Club Drive (now Olympic Boulevard) to the south was McCarthy Vista Parkway, in the center of which was to be located a Pacific Electric Railway streetcar station. McCarthy also planned a shopping center of eighteen stores that would overlook a landscape of ornamental lagoons, a movie theater, a school and a hotel.

Carthay Center Elementary School, located at 6351 Olympic Boulevard, opened in 1926 in a building designed by Horatio W. Bishop and Carleton M. Winslow, who were also the overall architects of the Carthay Center development. Because Miracle Mile was not yet developed, Carthay's was among a handful of commercial centers planned between Western Avenue and Beverly Hills. Planning for public transportation to link this neighborhood to downtown was one of its selling points. An important feature of the layout of Carthay Center, still preserved, was its irregular street pattern interspersed with pedestrian walkways. McCarthy's interests in developing the community were didactic, as well as commercial. A short biographical notice on him published in 1926 emphasized his desire to preserve the history of California where possible. He named the streets of Carthay Center after early state pioneers and commissioned art for the Carthay movie theater that would reflect on various events in the history of the state. McCarthy also commissioned a bronze statue in memory of the men of the gold rush that was modeled after his father. Currently, the boundaries of Carthay Center are defined by Schumacher Drive to the west,

Carthay Theatre, constructed in 1926 and demolished in 1969, seen here in a 1940 photograph. *Courtesy of "Dick" Whittington.*

Fairfax Avenue to the east, Olympic Boulevard to the south and Wilshire Boulevard to the north. San Vicente Boulevard, which at that time was known as Eulalia Street, in honor of a Los Angeles midwife, crosses this area diagonally. Carthay Center, renamed Carthay Circle, was designated HPOZ in 1998.

Carthay Center's famed movie theater opened at 6316 San Vicente Boulevard in 1926, with a premier of Cecil B. DeMille's *The Volga Boatman*. Initial plans for the theater were prepared by the architect A.B. Rosenthal. Its exterior was designed by Carleton M. Winslow and Horatio W. Bishop in the Spanish Colonial Revival style. This was one of the most significant movie theaters in Los Angeles, and its tall tower illuminated by lights was a recognizable landmark. The theater was financed by J. Harvey McCarthy and one of his associates, Fred A. Miller. In keeping with the overall design of Carthay Center, McCarthy wanted the decorative scheme of the interior of Carthay Theatre to commemorate California's pioneers. Frank Tenney Johnson, a painter known for western themes, was commissioned to paint landmarks of early California history, with titles such as *The Eagle Theater of Sacramento, California's First Theater* and *The Arrival of the Donner Party*. The Pasadena artist Alson Clark was also engaged to work on a group of paintings for the mezzanine, on topics such as "The Founding of Los Angeles" and "The Arrival of Jedediah Strong Smith at San Gabriel Mission." The sculptor Henry Lion created a bronze statue for the lobby, called *California Sunshine*. Many movies had their premiers at the theater, among them Walt Disney's *Snow White and the Seven Dwarves*, which opened on December 21, 1937. The final movie to be shown here was *The Shoes of the Fisherman*, starring Anthony Quinn, which played in the summer of 1969. A few years earlier, in 1963, National General Corporation began redevelopment plans to include a $4 million office building and commercial center for this location. The 1,126-seat theater was demolished in 1969.

In his grand plan for Carthay Center, J. Harvey McCarthy included memorials to his friends and parents. Several of them are still extant. In 1923, McCarthy built the Amanda Chapel, dedicated to his mother, still located at 6301 Olympic Boulevard and used as a house of worship. A larger-than-life bronze statue of a Forty-Niner prospector holding a pan adorns the small park-like triangle on the north side of the intersection of San Vicente Boulevard and McCarthy Vista. This memorial commemorates Daniel McCarthy, the developer's father. It was designed by the sculptor Henry Lion and was supposedly modeled on a daguerreotype of Daniel McCarthy taken in 1850. The sculpture was once part of a fountain and had water falling from the prospector's pan. It was dedicated in 1925 by the Ramona Parlor 109 and still bears the inscription that states: "This fountain is a memorial to the gallant pioneers of '49 of whom Daniel O. McCarthy, patriot miner, leader, was an outstanding example. He was born Raleigh, N.C., August 24, 1830. Died Los Angeles, August 13, 1919. Through his newspaper

Memorial to Daniel O. McCarthy by Henry Lion, located on San Vicente Boulevard. Photographed in 2012. *Courtesy of Ruth Wallach.*

'The American Flag,' San Francisco, he helped preserve California to the Union. This long, useful life is a heritage of which the Golden State is justly proud." As the price of metal soared in the early part of the twenty-first century, the statue was stolen in early February 2008, sawn in two above the knees and trucked to a local metal scrap yard. It was recovered by the police about a week later and eventually reinstalled in its historic location.

Across San Vicente Boulevard from the statue of the Forty-Niner is another memorial designed by Henry Lion, located on a green plaza of the modern commercial building that stands where Carthay Theatre used to. Dedicated in 1926 by the Native Sons of the Golden West and the Los Angeles Historical Society, it depicts Juan Bautista de Anza. The accompanying text states: "Juan Bautista de Anza. Soldier, explorer and discoverer of the overland route from Sonora Mexico to California. Leader of the first Spanish settlers who came through San Carlos Pass December 1775 on the way to Monterrey."

The fourth remaining memorial is a boulder that features a plaque commemorating "Snowshoe" Thompson, the first letter carrier to cross the Sierras. The commemorative plaque reads: "A pioneer hero of the Sierras who for twenty winters carried the mail over the mountains to isolated camps rescuing the lost and giving succor to those in need along the way. Born 1827 Died 1876." The boulder is located on a green lawn just northeast of the Carthay Center elementary school, near Commodore Sloat Drive, although this may not have been its original site. In 1926, when the boulder was dedicated to Thompson, a Sequoia tree was planted in his memory nearby. Another large boulder that commemorated Jedediah Strong Smith,

44

Right: Bust of Juan Bautista de Anza by Henry Lion, located on the site of Carthay Theatre. Photographed in 2013. *Courtesy of Ruth Wallach*.

Below: Boulder and plaque commemorating "Snowshoe" Thompson, the first letter carrier to cross the Sierras. Located in Carthay Circle. Photographed in 2013. *Courtesy of Ruth Wallach*

the first Anglo to enter California by an overland route, was installed at Carthay Center's commercial area in 1926. It came from a location near the trail that Smith followed into California and weighed thirteen tons. This boulder's whereabouts are unknown.

McCarthy also commissioned a sundial, which was installed at the commercial center of the subdivision in 1925 in memory of his friend Irwin J. Muma, an insurance company executive and a local civic and educational leader. The sundial was designed by Horatio W. Bishop and constructed of brick from the San Juan Capistrano Mission. Its whereabouts are also unknown. Lastly, although not directly related to McCarthy, the 1941 Works Progress Administration guide to Los Angeles also listed a Chinese peach tree on the esplanade of San Vicente Boulevard, which was presented by the Chinese consul at the premier of the movie *The Good Earth* at the Carthay Theatre in 1937.

I have described some of the residential developments on Wilshire Boulevard that extended the city's limits from Western and Crenshaw Avenues westward to Miracle Mile and beyond because they provide a context to A.W. Ross's plans for developing a commercial center here. When Ross is purported to have drawn a circle centered on this section of Wilshire Boulevard, it did not just reach neighborhoods located four or five miles away, such as Hollywood, Westlake Park or Beverly Hills. It also contained within its boundaries Windsor Park, Wilshire Crest and other new neighborhoods described in this chapter. Almost all, with the exception of Carthay Center, which in its plans boasted the only commercial center west of Western Avenue, were developed strictly as residential tracts. Miracle Mile was well positioned to serve their banking and shopping needs.

MIRACLE MILE: AN IDEA WITHOUT BOUNDARIES

As soon as Ross and his associates were able to rezone their tracts on Wilshire Boulevard for commercial development, Miracle Mile began to grow quickly. In the early 1920s, streets crossing Wilshire Boulevard in the Mile, such as Hauser Boulevard, were laid out and paved. Advertisements began to appear in the Los Angeles newspapers in the late 1920s publicizing opportunities to invest in Miracle Mile frontage. Investors were wooed with promises that land prices would go up rapidly because improvements were planned on the lots. A typical advertisement from 1929 read: "Thirteen investors answered this 'ad' last week on Wilshire and Hauser. They offered other property in part payment. It's difficult to trade Gold Dollars for worn-out coppers, but the man who gets this 70 feet at our price will be the winner." La Brea Avenue on the Mile's east side rapidly developed as an important traffic artery, and by the late 1920s, it was entirely paved between Pico and Santa Monica Boulevards. By 1928, it was reported that the intersection of La Brea and Wilshire was the third heaviest automobile corner in Los Angeles. Wilshire Boulevard at Miracle Mile became so congested with car and pedestrian traffic that there were intermittent plans to build pedestrian subways under it.

Ross quickly attracted major downtown-based clothing retailers and banks to construct or lease buildings on Miracle Mile. Beginning with the late 1920s, as Desmond's, Silverwood's, Security-First National Bank and Ralphs grocery store established branches on Miracle Mile, many other businesses began to consider doing the same. Although streetcars were still an important means of transportation in the city, and advertisements for some of the newly developed tracts provided directions for tourists coming by rail, Miracle Mile was an early example of a commercial center catering to customers who traveled by automobile. In part, this had to do with its location, initially outside city limits. In part, as has been stated elsewhere, Miracle Mile's development was oriented to automobile travel. While the Dominguez, Wilshire Tower and E. Clem Wilson Buildings conformed to the height-limit ordinance that was in effect until the late 1950s, their imposing Art Deco towers and business signage functioned as signposts for those traveling by car. From the beginning, Miracle Mile businesses offered parking that was considered ample by the standards of the 1920s and 1930s. Every time construction of a new building was announced, parking was part of the publicity. In the earlier days, parking lots were located behind the Wilshire Boulevard frontage. Later in the twentieth century, new construction began including parking as part of the structure.

The Mile's commercial history is not merely confined to the big retailers and banks that have left their indelible mark on architecture, surviving signage and historic photographs. It also attracted smaller chains and specialty shops, some, but not all, of which were rooted in downtown. In 1928, Ross signed one of the oldest sporting goods companies in Los Angeles, Cline & Cline, to lease a plot on the northeast corner of Wilshire Boulevard and Cloverdale Avenue and construct a two-story building. The same year, Ross began developing the southwest corner of Wilshire and Hauser Boulevards for Charles E. Cooper, his partner and a real estate holder in the Los Angeles and San Diego areas. The proposed structure was to contain stores, apartments and a car garage. By the 1930s, this block also included a bank, although no apartments were built. Following the by-now-established trend of retail and commerce moving westward from downtown, Brown's Mercantile, a men's apparel store, opened its second location on this corner in mid-November 1948. And so it went.

By the late 1930s, Miracle Mile east of Hauser Boulevard was considerably built up, with many commercial signs dotting the landscape. There were branches of Coulter's and Woolworth's department stores, banks, automotive businesses, two movie theaters, shoe stores, men's and women's clothing stores, food markets such as A&P and Ralphs and eateries like the Melody Lane Café and the White Spot Café. By the early 1960s, the entire stretch of Miracle Mile boasted four large department stores: May Company, The Broadway (which was located in the former Coulter's building), Seibu (a Japanese department store) and Ohrbach's. There were apparel stores catering to men, such as Mullen & Bluett, Phelps-Terkel and Zachary All; jewelers, including Donavan & Seamans, purported to be the oldest jewelry store in Los Angeles; three radio stations;

A typical view from circa 1950 showing the densely developed Miracle Mile east of Hauser Boulevard. *Courtesy of "Dick" Whittington.*

major insurance companies such as Prudential and Mutual of Omaha; eight banks, among them Bank of America, Citizen's National and California Federal; numerous advertising firms; and restaurants. All commercial establishments continued facing Wilshire Boulevard but provided ample parking and major entrances in the back.

By 1941, all of the property along Wilshire Boulevard in the Miracle Mile area was rezoned for commercial use. Ross continued his active involvement in Miracle Mile until his death in 1968. He envisioned the Mile as much more than a commercial stretch, although many of his ideas did not come to fruition. Already in the 1920s, Ross had particular plans for the expansion of Miracle Mile. In 1929, he wanted to build a forty-story hotel for $5 million, to be located on Wilshire Boulevard near Ogden Drive, and asked the architect Kenneth MacDonald to prepare some sketches. Because Miracle Mile was located outside city limits, Ross and his partner in this venture, Charles E. Cooper, felt that the building did not have to conform to the height-limit ordinance. To improve foot traffic and car circulation, Ross proposed to build five pedestrian tunnels under Wilshire Boulevard west of La Brea Avenue, for which he claimed to have the agreement of 85 percent of property owners.

This photograph from 1929 shows the sketch for a hotel development that Kenneth MacDonald drew for A.W. Ross. The hotel was to be located on the corner of Wilshire Boulevard and Ogden Drive but was never built. *Courtesy of the* Examiner.

Although neither the tunnels nor the hotel were built, they were part of a larger planning process in which Ross was engaged. In 1929, he announced a five-year construction program, during the course of which he proposed to erect "500 hotels and apartment houses" at a cost of $50 million. Under consideration were the two hundred acres owned by George Allan Hancock, dotted with oil derricks and bounded by Wilshire Boulevard to the south, Third Street to the north, La Brea Avenue to the east and Fairfax Avenue to the west. A man of grand vision, Ross declared that this area north of Wilshire Boulevard

> *will be the concentration point of Western Los Angeles' retail-buying power. In this connection we are stressing the fact that Hancock will open up the 200 acres he owns west of La Brea as a subdivision in 1930. At that date the present oil leases on the acreage will have expired, and the property is being planned as a mecca for high-class apartment houses, hotels, and semipublic buildings. Great garages are being erected in the center of this property west of La Brea to house the automobiles.*

Ross's plans do not appear to have come to fruition, at least not in the way he envisioned them. For one, the Great Depression intervened. In addition, much of the surrounding acreage, particularly to the north, was owned by others, whose interests did not entirely diverge from Ross's yet also did not neatly dovetail into his plans. Already in 1915, a decade before Miracle Mile began developing, George Allan Hancock, known not just for his ownership of Rancho La Brea and his business acumen but also for his civic mindedness and his interests in culture and the sciences, donated thirty acres fronting Wilshire Boulevard to Los Angeles County for a park. The land became known as Hancock Park (not to be confused with the residential subdivision of the same name farther east, also located on Hancock lands) and eventually became home to the George C. Page Museum at the La Brea Tar Pits and the Los Angeles County Museum of Art. Hancock began selling the Wilshire Boulevard frontage of the former Rancho La Brea in the mid-1920s to some of Ross's clients. In November 1923, he subdivided part of his land to the north of Wilshire and had it zoned for multifamily development. Oil derricks remained here until around 1940, at which point the land was soon redeveloped into a district with garden apartments and residential towers known as Parklabrea.

Parklabrea (also spelled as Park Labrea and Park La Brea) is a residential development located on approximately 176 acres north of Miracle Mile, between Sixth Street to the south, Third Street to the north, Fairfax Avenue to the west and Cochran Avenue to the east. It was constructed by Metropolitan Life Insurance Company beginning in 1941 as a moderate-cost rental housing project on land that George Allan Hancock initially donated to the University of Southern California (USC) in 1939. This was the remainder of what was once Rancho La Brea. Metropolitan Life Insurance Company purchased the land from USC in 1940 for approximately $1.5 million and planned to invest another $13 million into construction of housing. This multifamily residential project was part of several programs of the federal government to encourage construction of dwellings for moderate-income families and to house the growing population of wartime workers. The development of Parklabrea also benefitted from the California state legislature allowing life insurance companies that operated in the state to invest in moderate-cost housing. Metropolitan Life contended that it has long been interested in housing projects in which private capital could economically invest in low-cost rentals.

The Parklabrea housing development was fiercely opposed by local apartment building owners and by some insurance policy holders, and the battle reached the state Supreme Court in 1940. After the court quickly ruled in favor of Metropolitan Life, the City of Los Angeles announced plans to annex this unincorporated land in order to expedite groundbreaking for construction. Work on the development began in late May 1941, at which point the public works and planning committees of city council made provisions to extend Hauser Boulevard northward as an artery passing through Parklabrea. The ordinance annexing the land to the city was adopted in July 1941.

During the first phase of construction, which was interrupted during World War II, Parklabrea consisted of thirty-one two-story garden apartments designed by the New York architect Leonard Schultze in association with the Los Angeles architect Earl T. Heitschmidt in a modernized American Colonial Revival style. The New York–based firm Starrett Bros. & Eiken did the construction. The apartment complexes were set around interior green commons. As befits the architectural style, entrances to the two-story apartments were framed by slender, tall columns. The garden apartments faced into the interior courtyards. Initial plans for Parklabrea called for 2,700 rentable units, outdoor-use facilities and thirty tennis courts set around a central recreational area. Only 18 percent of the land was supposed to go toward housing, the rest of the acreage providing a park-like setting.

By 1945, Metropolitan Life succeeded in completing about half of the planned development. Foundations were laid for the remainder, and construction was temporarily suspended until the late1940s. In 1948–49, Parklabrea began expanding eastward, with Metropolitan Life financing eighteen apartment structures of thirteen stories each, to the tune of about $30 million. This expansion increased the number of apartments from the 1,380 that were initially built to 4,400. The new high-rise buildings were designed by Leonard Schultze, architect of the earlier garden apartments, in association with the Los Angeles–based architectural firm of Kaufmann & Stanton. Garage structures were built for each of the towers. Starrett Bros. & Eiken again did the construction work, and Thomas Church planned the landscaping. Unlike the older garden apartments on the property, all apartments in the X-shaped towers faced outward. The expanded Parklabrea opened to occupancy in 1950.

Parklabrea's overall street plan is in the shape of a diamond connected to two octagons on its east and west via circular plazas. Diagonal streets radiate from the diamond and the octagons, creating a grid that is entirely distinct from the mainly gridiron pattern of the surrounding streets. This layout

The street layout of Parklabrea, with its garden and high-rise apartments, is seen in this aerial photograph from 1954. *Courtesy of "Dick" Whittington.*

makes the residential development a self-contained environment. Set within carefully landscaped areas are the original two-story garden apartments, mostly located on the west side of Parklabrea, and the post–World War II thirteen-story residential towers, mostly located on its east side. Given their height, the apartment towers were sometimes called dragon teeth protruding above the generally low-rise Los Angeles skyline.

In addition to housing, Metropolitan Life also made plans for an open-air shopping center, which was designed by Stiles O. Clements. It was laid out in 1953 on the southwest corner of Third Street and Ogden Drive and extended westward toward Fairfax Avenue. The original design of the shopping center included a deep setback south from Third Street for a parking area to accommodate approximately one thousand cars. It included a large food market, a drugstore and a Van de Kamp's bakery. The shopping center, although somewhat altered, is still extant, currently accommodating a variety of businesses, as well as a CVS Pharmacy, a K-Mart and a Whole Foods market. By 1955, Barraclough restaurant, built by P.J. Walker, opened on Third Street just east of the shopping mall to serve the residents of Parklabrea and the surrounding residential communities. From the 1970s into the 1980s, Parklabrea was managed jointly by Metropolitan Life and May Company. In the 1980s, although crime rate was low at the housing complex, overall security became one of the top issues for the elderly residents, who composed approximately half of its population. In 1983, Parklabrea obtained permission from the city to close access to its streets. Today, it is completely gated.

There were other real estate holders with investments in Miracle Mile and its environs. The Evans Ferguson Corporation, headed by Hugh Evans and Harold Gale Ferguson, invested in lots on the southeast corner of Wilshire and La Brea. In 1923, Evans Ferguson purchased 285 acres of land bordering the northwest corner of Wilshire and Fairfax, where Rogers Airport used to be. The company established its offices in this area and named the property the Wilshire-Fairfax tract. The land was quickly improved with sidewalks, landscaping and drainage. Mains for gas, water and electricity were installed. Almost immediately, it was subdivided for sale, with the majority of the lots sold off within a year. Within the next few years, single-family homes and small apartment houses were built on the lots.

The Gilmore Oil Company owned 256 acres around Fairfax Avenue and Third Street. The company and its principal owner, Earl B. Gilmore, were instrumental in shaping the built landscape of this area. Several institutions established through the Gilmore investments still exist. One of them is

Farmer's market, photographed circa 1953. Its iconic clock tower is seen to the right. The grove of trees in the background marks the current location of the Grove shopping center. *Courtesy of CHS.*

the Farmer's Market. In 1933, Earl B. Gilmore backed a proposal from a bookkeeper named Roger Dahlhjelm to establish a farmer's market on 20 acres located on the northeast corner of Fairfax Avenue and Third Street. The market opened in 1934 with the purpose of giving local dairy farmers and fruit and vegetable growers a place to sell fresh produce during the Great Depression. While the market's origins were part of Gilmore's benevolence and largess, he was a businessman first and foremost. Farmers initially leased stalls for fifty cents a day, and by the end of the decade, the market proved to be a successful profit-making venture. After renovation and expansion in 1941, the market's Clock Tower became a recognizable landmark that appeared in advertisements and photographs.

In 1934, Earl Gilmore built a racetrack for midget car races, which were one of his passions. It became known as Gilmore Stadium. Located on the southeast corner of Fairfax Avenue and Beverly Boulevard, the stadium was a wooden structure that seated eighteen thousand people. In

This circa 1940 photograph looking northwest shows Gilmore Stadium (left) and Gilmore Baseball Field (right). CBS Television City is located on the site of the Gilmore fields. *Courtesy of the* Examiner.

addition to midget car races, it hosted football games (it was home to the Bulldogs, purportedly the first professional football team in Los Angeles) and other forms of sports entertainment. A few years later, in 1938, Gilmore Baseball Stadium, more popularly known as Gilmore Field, was constructed somewhat southeast of Gilmore Stadium. Gilmore Field was home to the Pacific Coast League's Hollywood Stars, a baseball team that was co-owned by Bing Crosby, Barbara Stanwyck and Cecil B. DeMille. Gilmore Stadium was razed in 1952, and Gilmore Field was razed in 1958. In 1948, the Gilmore Drive-In movie theater was built on the south side of Pan Pacific Park, at 6201 Third Street, with capacity for 650 cars. It operated until the mid-1970s and was razed soon thereafter.

As the economy began to emerge from the Great Depression, the Gilmore Oil Company considered additional investments into its property. In 1940, it planned to build a large one-story shopping mall of seventy-five thousand square feet on the portion of the acreage called Gilmore Island, adjacent to the Farmer's Market. The preliminary design in the English Gothic architectural style was called Gilmore Village Store, with space for sixty stores. To accommodate anticipated increased traffic for both the mall and the Farmer's Market, the plan included an extensive parking area. This development was thwarted by World War II, although eventually more permanent structures were built around the parking lot just north of the Farmer's Market.

While the start of World War II delayed the plans for Gilmore Village, the war revived the oil business, which was beginning to fade in the 1930s. In 1942, city council passed several ordinances to permit drilling for oil on Gilmore Island, advancing the argument that this was needed to boost the war effort. The ordinances allowed the city to annex this plot of nineteen acres, previously located on unincorporated land, and permitted the construction of a pipeline to the beach, operated by Shell Oil. Concerned residential property owners to the north were told that drilling operations would be housed in a building of architectural beauty so as not to detract from the value of their properties. Incidentally, both Gilmore Stadium and Gilmore Field were exempt from annexation to the city.

There was an economic reason for the demolition of Gilmore Stadium and Gilmore Field. In 1950, the Columbia Broadcasting System (CBS) negotiated the purchase of the plot on which the stadium stood to erect its West Coast headquarters for television production. The architects William L. Pereira and Charles Luckman did the master planning of a twenty-five-acre site for what became known as CBS Television City. Included in the master plan were fifteen acres of Gilmore Island that CBS already purchased, as well as the site of the Gilmore baseball park, which became available in 1958 after the occupancy contract with the Hollywood Stars expired. The building complex for CBS opened in 1952, with more facilities added in the late 1950s on the site of the baseball park. The architects' design for the main complex was based on the modernist cube of starkly contrasted black and white surfaces, with slender structural columns framing ribbons of windows. Despite the master planning and the boosterism, CBS Television City did not become the television capital, as was presumed in the 1950s, because the company consolidated its television headquarters in New York in the following decade.

It is impossible to discuss developments adjacent to Miracle Mile without mentioning Pan Pacific Auditorium. The auditorium was designed by the architecture firm of Walter Wurdeman and Welton Becket in 1934. When it opened in 1935, the building, noted for its four Streamline Moderne fin-shaped towers above the front, stood out against a backdrop of oil wells of Gilmore

Photograph of the master plan for CBS Television City by William L. Pereira and Charles Luckman, 1950. *Courtesy of the* Examiner.

Island. The first event that took place at the Pan Pacific was a sixteen-day model home exhibition that featured, among others, the architect Wallace Neff's honeymoon cottage, which was also a mobile home. Pan Pacific Auditorium was owned by Errett Lobban Cord and later by his son, Charles, and had a seating capacity of up to ten thousand people. Over the thirty-seven years of its existence, the auditorium was a site of sports events, concerts, roller derbies and an occasional political rally. Elvis Presley's first appearance on the West Coast was held here. By the 1970s, it regularly put up three annual shows: the Boat Show, the Sportsmen Show and the Automobile Show.

Facing competition from newer and larger entertainment centers, as well as from the large convention center in downtown Los Angeles, the auditorium closed in 1972. In 1979, after several years of advocacy, the parcel surrounding it was designated a regional park, to be developed jointly by Los Angeles County and the City of Los Angeles. The architecture firm of Walter Gruen Associates developed plans for the twenty-eight-acre site that was still unincorporated. The park, which also doubled as a flood control basin, was finally inaugurated in 1983. By 1984, there were plans to turn the site of the Pan Pacific Auditorium, which was empty and suffered from neglect and fires, into a 142-room hotel and an office complex with two theaters. Because Pan Pacific Auditorium was listed on the National Register of Historic Places, its façade was supposed to be preserved and incorporated into the commercial structure. The redevelopment proposal was approved in part to generate funds for the maintenance of the park in a post–Proposition 13 climate of reduced tax revenues. The redevelopment of the auditorium did not take place, however, and it completely burned down in 1989.

The Pan Pacific Park Recreation Center, dedicated on the site of Pan Pacific Auditorium in 2002, was designed by Jeffrey M. Kalban & Associates to pay homage to the original building, particularly in the placement of a fin-shaped tower over the entrance. To commemorate the bygone era in architecture represented by Pan Pacific Auditorium, the recreation building's exterior and lobby walls feature photographic tiles that depict examples of noted Art Deco architectural gems in Los Angeles. The ghosts of Pan Pacific Auditorium, Gilmore Stadium and other historic sites on the Wilshire-

Detail of the wall tiles that decorate the recreation building located on the site of Pan Pacific Auditorium. The tiles show famous Art Deco architectural details, including the fin-shaped towers of the auditorium, as well as the tower of Desmond's store. Photographed in 2013. *Courtesy of Ruth Wallach.*

View of the Los Angeles Holocaust Monument located in Pan Pacific Park, photographed in 2013. The monument's design has been altered to better integrate it with the façade of the Holocaust Museum, seen to the left. *Courtesy of Ruth Wallach.*

Fairfax tracts are also commemorated in a mural and stained glass designed in 2005 by Joyce Dallal for the Fairfax branch of the Los Angeles Public Library, located at 161 Gardner Street nearby.

In addition to paying homage to Pan Pacific Auditorium and early twentieth-century architecture, the park has several public art works and a museum. The Los Angeles Holocaust Monument, located on the northwest side of the park, was designed in the early 1990s by Dr. Joseph L. Young. The monument is composed of six eighteen-foot-tall triangular columns of black granite arranged in a circular pattern on a plaza. They are symbolic of the smokestacks of crematoria of Nazi concentration camps. The sides of each column have informational panels describing Holocaust-related historic events that occurred from 1933 to 1945. The open space in the middle of the monument was emblematic of the seventh column, in reference to those who survived the Holocaust. According to Dr. Young's design, there was to be a "Flame of Memory" on top of each column, burning for twenty-four hours during Holocaust Remembrance Day each year. Originally, the columns stood on a red plaza, symbolizing the blood of those

Seen in this 2013 photograph is the 1943 statue by Robert Paine of Haym Solomon. It is located in Pan Pacific Park. *Courtesy of Ruth Wallach.*

who died. The stairs leading to the columns were painted black and white, connoting the railroad tracks that carried victims to their deaths in concentration camps and gas chambers. The fundraising campaign to build the monument was sponsored by the American Congress of Jews from Poland and Survivors of Concentration Camps. The site was selected, in part, because it was easily accessible by car and public transportation and was located in an area with a heavy concentration of Jewish population from Eastern and Central Europe. The architecture firm Nadel Partnership constructed the monument with contractor Goldrich & Kest, and it was dedicated on April 26, 1992.

For some years, the monument was surrounded by a fence in order to ward off vandalism. Eighteen years later, in 2010, the Los Angeles Holocaust Museum opened immediately to the north of the memorial. Designed by the architect Hagy Belzberg, the smoothly curving, exposed concrete structure is partially sunk in the ground and is topped by an earthen roof where drought-resistant plants grow. The plaza on which the memorial stands was redesigned in order to visually open up the space for the Holocaust Museum. Curving concrete pathways, mimicking the exterior of the museum, now lead to the monument, replacing the black and white stairs. The wall of red panels that originally surrounded the monument is also gone. Another memorial of relevance to Jewish history is located on the southeast side of the park near the intersection of Third and Gardner Streets. This statue from 1943, designed by Robert Paine, commemorates the eighteenth-century Jewish American patriot Haym Solomon. Originally sited in Hollenbeck Park, then in MacArthur Park, the statue was moved to the east side of Pan Pacific Park in 1984. It has been in its current location since 2008.

Chapter 3

MODERN ARCHITECTURE AND POSTWAR REDEVELOPMENT

In the previous chapter, I discussed the place of Miracle Mile and its environs in the overall pattern of residential and commercial growth of Los Angeles along Wilshire Boulevard toward Beverly Hills. The evolution of the Mile, whose geographic borders must by necessity be more broadly defined than originally designated, was also part of historic trends in architecture, post–World War II urban redevelopment and evolution of urban transportation.

Modern Housing

By 1935, several businessman and commercial property owners, among them A.W. Ross; E. Clem Wilson, who financed one of Miracle Mile's most iconic extant buildings; and John O'Melveny, partner in an important Los Angeles law firm, formed the Miracle Mile Business Men's Association to further economic and residential growth on Wilshire Boulevard and in the surrounding areas. The association's chairman, Ralph Huesman, owner of Desmond's stores, proclaimed in a typically boosterist fashion, "A little more than ten years ago, two or three old ranch houses looming over barley fields were all you could see here." Not content with overseeing the birth of Miracle Mile, the association continued planning for the Mile's expansion, which early on included plans to construct a million-dollar Federal Armory and to host a variety of public events to attract more attention to the district. The armory did not materialize, but some of the public events, particularly those promoting residential architecture and innovative housing, did.

The success of Miracle Mile partly rested on the rapid growth of nearby residential tracts. Already by the late 1920s, small multifamily apartment homes were constructed to the north and south of Wilshire Boulevard. Many of the lots within the radius of a mile were built up with single-family homes by the late 1940s. The commercial architecture of the Mile itself at that time tended toward variations of Spanish Colonial Revival, Art Deco and Streamline Moderne. The residential developments reflected period revival architecture common for this time period, such as Spanish Colonial, American Colonial, English, French and Mediterranean Revival styles. However, the building of the residential tracts, the bulk of which occurred in the 1920s and 1930s, coincided with the introduction of Modernism into Los Angeles architecture. This was both a reflection of the presence here of Bauhaus-influenced and European-trained architects and of the role of the curriculum of the School of Architecture at the University of Southern California in disseminating modern design and utilitarianism in architectural practice. The environs of Miracle Mile contain several residential buildings designed in the Modernist style, located within a mile to the south. On the southwest corner of Genesee and Eighth Streets, about a block south of Wilshire Boulevard, is the Buck House, designed by Rudolph Schindler in 1934. Situated on a triangular plot, its plan is composed of two adjoining L shapes that frame two inner courtyards. The house has varying ceiling heights, rooflines and exterior volumes that contextualize its interior spaces. The absence of a straight and flat roofline is typical of Schindler's work and a reason for why he was not included in the architectural canon of International Modernism. The rooms open onto an interior patio, which provides them with natural light through floor-to-ceiling fenestration. As is the case with other architectural work by Schindler, clerestory windows are an additional source of natural light for the interior and make the ceiling appear to float above the walls. Given Schindler's interest in designing single-family homes that have an additional source of income, this house also includes a small, rentable apartment.

Less than a mile farther south is another building by Rudolph Schindler, the Pearl M. Mackey Apartments, located on the northwest corner of Cochran Avenue and Edgewood Place, finished in 1939. The four compact apartments have their own private outdoor living areas, either in the form of a patio or as a roof garden. The apartments (one of them is a penthouse) have clerestory windows and perforated interior walls that allow natural light to permeate all interior spaces, as is typical of Schindler's work.

The Buck House, designed by Rudolph Schindler in 1934, located immediately south of Miracle Mile, is seen in this 2011 photograph. *Courtesy of Ruth Wallach.*

Photographed here in 2011 is the Pearl M. Mackey apartment house designed by Rudolph Schindler in 1939. *Courtesy of Ruth Wallach.*

The Dunsmuir Flats apartment building, designed by Gregory Ain in 1937, is seen on the left. Photographed in 2012. *Courtesy of Ruth Wallach.*

The rectangular exterior is composed of L shaped forms that frame large expanses of glass and jutting, interlocking volumes. The building is owned by the MAK Center for Art and Architecture, Los Angeles, and is used as living quarters for MAK's artists in residence.

Somewhat farther south, on Dunsmuir Avenue north of Packard Street, is a four-unit apartment house designed by Gregory Ain in 1937 known as Dunsmuir Flats. It is set on a narrow, sloping site, as are almost all the other dwellings on this street, many of which are small apartment homes designed in more traditional styles. Dunsmuir Flats is composed of four staggered rectangles. As Sam Hall Kaplan aptly wrote in his 1988 *Los Angeles Times* article "Ain's Contributions Remembered," the architect "manipulated the cubist-styled units to create an open, informal plan focused on a row of private gardens." Ain's goal was to provide light from three sides for all rooms in the two-story apartments through use of clerestories, windows and trellised balconies. He used the rising grade of the property to place the enclosed gardens one above the other.

These three buildings were not entirely an anomaly for Miracle Mile, although Modernist architectural style did not become prevalent in residential architecture here. Miracle Mile, and its environs, was a site for exhibitions of modern architecture that highlighted improvements in building and household technologies. They were part of the evolution of developer- and architect-planned communities that were built in Los Angeles and elsewhere partly in response to the minimum standards for housing advocated by the federal government. The intent of such exhibitions was to demonstrate what the federal government, housing organizations and the building industry considered examples of good dwellings that improved housekeeping. They were part of a broad national movement to spread the message of homeownership through demonstration homes, lectures, architectural competitions and various publications authored by government agencies and private developers. The intent of such publications was to inform the general public of the practical details of home architecture and construction, as well as of the processes involved in the purchase and financing of family dwellings. Manufacturers, department stores, and utility companies participated in outfitting the showcase homes with the latest appliances and furnishings. The *Los Angeles Times* often sponsored such shows, particularly to demonstrate low- to medium-cost houses, during which a home would be raffled as a prize. Pan Pacific Auditorium, located just north of the Mile on Beverly Boulevard, hosted some of the demonstration home and household improvement shows.

An outdoor show of modern homes that ran for a long time took place on Miracle Mile in 1936–37. Organized by Marie Louise Schmidt, who oversaw the Architects' Building Materials exhibitions in downtown Los Angeles and, with her sister, wrote construction advice columns in the *Los Angeles Times*, the show was called "The California House and Garden Exhibition." It was located at 5900 Wilshire Boulevard, between Spaulding Avenue and Genesee Street, opposite what is today the campus of the Los Angeles County Museum of Art. The exhibition was sponsored by the Los Angeles Chamber of Commerce, the Federal Housing Administration and various local civic and garden clubs. Its purpose was to demonstrate six types of low-cost, middle-class homes. Close to two hundred manufacturers, interior decorators and landscape architects contributed materials and labor. Each of the original six homes was designed by a local architect in different styles, and all construction costs had to be under $5,000, a figure seen as just about affordable for a middle-class family. Tens of thousands of people visited the exhibition during the first six months, with nominal admission fees going toward reimbursing the dealers.

Schmidt's idea was to make the exhibition long term and showcase different products over time. To this end, the organizers held a periodic contest among the visitors, the winner getting one of the houses, which was then moved away and replaced by a new one, designed in a different style. The participating builders and manufacturers also came up with their own plans to keep public interest, holding monthly breakfasts for the exhibitors, occasional fashion shows, a badminton tournament, garden parties and several radio broadcasts. The outdoor exhibition was designed as a hamlet with its own temporary streets. In the center of the hamlet was a landscaped plaza-like area that contained some public seating, with the demonstration homes, exhibition spaces and administrative facilities built around it. The houses constructed for the original display were as follows: a California cottage by the architect Winchton L. Risley and interior decorator Harry Gladstone; a New Orleans–style house by the architects John Byers and Edla Muir in association with interior decorators Cannell & Chaffin, Inc.; a Moderne house, also known as Plywood house, by Richard J. Neutra; an English cottage by Arthur Kelly and Joe Estep; a French-style house by Paul R. Williams; and an Economy cottage by Gordon Kaufmann and Allen G. Siple. Gardens for the houses were designed by Hammond Sadler, Charles G. Adams, Ralph D. Cornell, Seymour Thomas, Edward Huntsman Trout and George Kern.

The architects used various current construction technologies. Paul Williams used a steel frame with plaster exterior for his French-style house. Kelly and Estep's English cottage was built of reinforced grout-lock brick masonry, and Risley constructed the California cottage from hollow concrete building tile. Richard Neutra's house was the most modernist, both in design and in its use of plywood. It was purported to be a smaller version of an earlier plywood house Neutra designed, which won second prize in the General Electric Small House Competition held the previous year. A practice at the Miracle Mile exhibition was to leave a portion of each house uncovered to show hidden materials. Where this was not possible, materials were displayed in an arcade adjoining the administration building. The architect Gordon B. Kaufmann designed the concrete wall separating the hamlet from Wilshire Boulevard.

At the conclusion of the first stage of the exhibition in October 1936, Winchton Risley's California cottage, with its enclosed patio, was voted favorite by the visitors, followed by the English cottage, the New Orleans house, the Moderne house, the French house and the Economy cottage, in that order. Additional designs were displayed in 1937. Among them was a California home suitable for year-round desert living designed by Lyle Nelson Barcume, and the "Colonel Evans Package House," a dwelling that

The interior of Fritz Burns's Postwar House, designed by Wurdeman and Becket, is seen in this 1948 photograph. *Courtesy of "Dick" Whittington.*

could be sold completely over-the-counter, manufactured by the Economy Housing Corporation. The houses and plans displayed at the exhibition ranged from about one thousand to three thousand square feet in size and cost between $4,000 and $10,000. The Colonel Evans Package House was the cheapest, marketed at a cost of under $3,000. The exhibition closed in early 1938. The Schmidt sisters continued penning their popular weekly "Construction Primer" column in the *Los Angeles Times* for the duration of the exhibition, to which they often made references.

Los Angeles experienced a great demand for housing, particularly in the immediate post–World War II period. Real estate developers, among them Fritz B. Burns, president of Henry J. Kaiser Homes, offered many modern amenities in standard prefabrication. To promote new housing technologies, Burns sponsored a noteworthy home exhibition on the eastern edge of the Miracle Mile area soon after the end of World War II. His Postwar House was constructed on the southeast corner of Wilshire Boulevard and Highland Avenue, at 4950 Wilshire, and opened to the public in 1946. The house was a collaborative project between Burns and the architects Walter Wurdeman and Welton Becket. Its purpose was to incorporate building materials and technologies that developed during World War II and to promote a residential lifestyle that showcased their use.

The Postwar House cost what for the time period was a whopping $175,000, with over one hundred manufacturers supplying products for it. Bullock's department store provided the furnishings. The house had the first electric garbage disposal, the first residential large-screen television, an automatic climate control system, two-way intercoms between all the rooms and other new domestic technologies. It had washable walls that could be easily wiped clean. Burns's employees displayed this feature with a dramatic gesture, smashing a bottle of ink against the white walls and then easily wiping them clean. Each room had full-height built-in closets, a feature that became standard in domestic interiors.

Burns, a noted local developer, established the Fritz B. Burns Research Division for Housing in 1943. The division studied the efficiency and viability of new materials for home construction and published advice for homeowners for care and repair of homes. Most importantly, it was a laboratory to try new products, materials, designs and methods of construction. Burns's core belief was that home buyers wanted to see familiar designs, in contrast to the innovative and modernist ideas that were practiced by the architects participating in the Case Study houses sponsored after World War II by John Entenza and the journal *Arts & Architecture*. Initially, entry into the Postwar House cost one dollar, and over one million people visited it in the next four or five years. The proceeds went to charitable organizations, particularly to St. Anne's Foundation and the St. Sophia Greek Orthodox Cathedral.

As public attendance declined, the Postwar House was redesigned into the House of Tomorrow by Welton Becket (Walter Wurdeman died in 1949) at the behest of Fritz Burns and reopened in 1951. Both the Postwar House and the House of Tomorrow were turned inward, focusing on the inner patio, in contrast to the more conventional frontal organization of most residential housing of the period. The 2,400-square-foot House of Tomorrow also promoted California's informal lifestyle and the permeability of indoor and outdoor spaces, both themes explored by many architects working in Southern California. Custom-made furniture in a contemporary French Provincial–inspired style was provided by Barker Bros. Other notable features included terraces for each of the bedrooms, a central garden that had radiant heating during the colder months and a kitchen that had a central island with a sink, a breakfast bar and economic storage for dishes.

The inner patio of the Postwar House functioned as the focal point for this house. Photographed circa 1946. *Courtesy of "Dick" Whittington.*

The front of Fritz Burns's House of Tomorrow, photographed in 2013. *Courtesy of Ruth Wallach.*

Every room had one wall made entirely of sliding glass. Also included in the one-dollar admission was the entry to the so-called Nutmeg House, a small two-bedroom cottage located on the same property near Highland Avenue. The House of Tomorrow was converted by Burns in the late 1950s into an office for his realty firm. In later years, it served various other organizations, including a private school, and still stands in this location, although considerably altered.

REVITALIZING THE DEAD MILE

Miracle Mile and its surrounding commercial and residential communities did not function on their own, exclusive of the economic and demographic waves that affected the Los Angeles region. From the late 1950s into the early 1970s, Wilshire Boulevard between Crenshaw and La Brea Avenues was occasionally dubbed the Dead Mile. Fifty-year deed restrictions limited its frontage to single-family developments and excluded commercial buildings that were over six stories high. In commercial real estate parlance, this rendered the stretch underdeveloped. Over time, attempts were made to change this and to densify Wilshire Boulevard from downtown to the sea, just as Ross dreamed. In 1959, in one such attempted project, the Los Angeles Archdiocese of the Catholic Church leased ten acres of land that it owned on the south side of Wilshire between Rimpau Boulevard and Tremaine Avenue to the New York banker George W. Warnecke. Warnecke hired the architecture firm of Charles Luckman Associates to develop plans for a city within a city, similar to Radio City in New York. Luckman's initial plan included a sixteen- to twenty-story hotel with 340 rooms, a twenty-two-story office building, a tall apartment building and several other smaller structures for stores, all linked by covered walkways. The plan, per Warnecke's specifications, also had rental apartments in the commercial structures, anticipating employees living and working on location. Part of this proposed $30 million project was also to develop a recreational park, as well as an underground garage for 3,400 cars. The archdiocese expected proceeds from the lease to go to its parochial schools, and Warnecke saw an opportunity to build a slice of New York–style dense living.

The plan was not realized, but its ideas did not vanish into oblivion. In 1964, the Wilshire-Fremont Corporation, composed of property owners in Fremont Place, proposed to rezone the neighborhood for the construction of twenty-one multistory apartment buildings along Wilshire Boulevard. According to the master plan developed by the architecture firm Welton Becket and Associates, the apartment buildings were to be thirteen to thirty stories in height with close to 4,700 apartments. The proposed development was valued at $200 million. The architects pledged to preserve Fremont Place's park-like atmosphere by generously spacing the high-rise buildings and surrounding them with landscaped gardens, swimming pools and broad plazas. The plans included curving roads, cul-de-sacs around the periphery and underground parking. While some Fremont Place property holders supported the rezoning efforts, many, including homeowners from the adjacent Hancock Park, Windsor Square and Oxford Square neighborhoods, did not. City council's planning committee denied the request for rezoning in early 1965.

When deed restrictions expired in 1971, the Los Angeles Planning Department and various developer groups started planning to convert the Dead Mile into a Park Mile. The new plans emphasized commercial and apartment buildings of twelve and fifteen stories in height, surrounded by abundant landscaping a block deep on both sides of Wilshire Boulevard, in order to provide a park-like buffer to adjacent residential neighborhood. At the same time, there were plans to remedy Wilshire Boulevard's massive traffic problems with mass rapid transit, such as rail, with stations located at major intersections. Other plans to alleviate traffic congestion called for remaking some streets into one-way and for the construction of the Beverly Hills Freeway to run north of the Wilshire residential tracts.

The proposed Park Mile high-rise developments and traffic-related plans proved controversial with the residential communities, which successfully fought them. Nevertheless, Wilshire Boulevard west of Crenshaw Avenue slowly changed to be lined with some commercial and cultural buildings, almost all of medium height and density. Most were built in the 1950s or later. The massive 1958 building, designed by Brandow & Johnson for Tidewater Oil Company at 4201 Wilshire Boulevard on the northwest corner with Crenshaw Avenue, is among the tallest. Over the years, this white marble-clad Modernist structure also came to house Getty Oil and, later, the Harbor Insurance Company.

The Scottish Rite Masonic Temple, at 4375 Wilshire Boulevard, is probably the most ornate of the buildings built in this period. It is located between Lucerne and Plymouth Boulevards on the north side of Wilshire. The temple is a massive Italianate structure built of marble, iron and steel. It was designed in 1960 by Millard O. Sheets, who also executed the exterior mosaics and painted the interior murals. Sheets personally selected the exterior marble and travertine from a quarry near Rome. Costing over $4 million to construct, the temple was completed in November 1961 and hailed as among the largest facilities of its kind in the United States. Its auditorium, designed for 1,700 people, was to have the same sound control system as Grauman's Chinese Theater in Hollywood, notable as among the most modern in the country. The foyer featured a mural by Sheets showing the history of freemasonry in California, with details on commerce, industry, transportation, agriculture and the judiciary system. For the auditorium, Sheets designed mosaic figures depicting various historic lawgivers. Sheets also designed the exterior mosaic on Plymouth Boulevard that shows various cities around the world symbolizing the universality of freemasonry: Jerusalem, Babylon, Acre, Rheims, Rome, Boston, London and Sacramento. The exterior mosaics on the façades facing Wilshire and Lucerne Boulevards represent various masonic symbols. There are also eight large sculptural groups decorating the temple's exterior. Fourteen feet in height, they are inscribed with names of important figures in the history of masonry. They were designed by the sculptor Albert Stewart, carved in travertine in Italy by Amleto Rossi and shipped from Rome to California. Additional decorative work, made of bronze, was also cast in Rome.

The interior of the temple was opened to the public at large for the first time four years after construction, in January 1965. In addition to the masonic lodge's activities, the temple was used for a variety of services, such as weddings and concerts. The Los Angeles Police Department used the temple for Special Weapons and Tactics team exercise and for funeral events. During the Los Angeles riots of 1992, the National Guard used the temple as a temporary barracks. The temple closed in April 1994 for financial reasons. Membership at this lodge declined in the 1970s and '80s after dispersing to other parts of the Greater Los Angeles area. At the same time, the Windsor Square Association brought the lodge before the zoning board. Although this lot was zoned for use by nonprofit and charitable organizations, the lodge began fundraising by renting the building out for commercial activities, which were not only at odds with zoning restrictions but also caused noise and parking problems. In 1994, when the Wilshire United Methodist Church across Wilshire Boulevard was devastated by fire, its services temporarily moved into the vacant temple. After the interior of the building was refurbished, its owners held several events there, which led to additional complaints from the neighborhood associations and to further hearings that eventually reached the California Supreme Court.

There are several other notable buildings on this stretch of Wilshire, dating from the mid- to late twentieth century. Among them is the Dunes Inn at 4300 Wilshire Boulevard, located on the southwest corner of the intersection with Windsor Boulevard. Designed in 1957 by Sam Reisbord, it is noted for its cylindrical corner tower and exterior tile cladding. Just east of the Scottish Rite Temple, on the northeast corner of Wilshire and Plymouth, at 4333 Wilshire Boulevard, is a bank building designed by William L. Pereira Associates in 1968, currently housing a J.P. Morgan Chase branch. The Hon-Michi Congregation Shutchosho Temple, at 4431–35 Wilshire Boulevard, was designed in 1984 by an architect named Obayashi.

The quick growth of Southern California in the

View of the exterior mosaic of the Scottish Rite Temple, designed by Millard Sheets in 1960. Photographed in 2011. *Courtesy of Ruth Wallach.*

post–World War II era resulted in the dispersal of commercial hubs, which developed their own "miracle miles" throughout the region. Demographic shifts included residential movement into the suburbs and the influx of African Americans—and eventually Koreans, Ethiopians, Latinos and other ethnic groups—into neighborhoods south and east of Miracle Mile. The success of Miracle Mile as a shopping and banking destination for those traveling by car was also its undoing. Miracle Mile was no longer unique, and some argued, it fell behind other such destinations. A 1970 report prepared by William L. Pereira Associates for the city's master planning of urban core centers stated:

73

Exterior sculptures designed by Albert Stewart decorate the Scottish Rite Temple. Photographed in 2011. *Courtesy of Ruth Wallach.*

View of Dunes Inn, designed by Sam Reisbord in 1957. Photographed in 2012. *Courtesy of Ruth Wallach.*

Until about 1952, the Miracle Mile area compared very favorably with other Los Angeles commercial districts. Growth in recent years, however, has been slower than that of most other commercial districts fronting on Wilshire Boulevard...Lack of well-known restaurants, entertainment facilities or hotel accommodations...are evidences of the weakness of the area as a well-balanced urban center.

The authors further noted that while Miracle Mile had several department stores, they were spaced far apart, and there was little of attractive commercial nature in between, except for office buildings and parking lots. Compared to suburban shopping malls, Miracle Mile by this period also lacked adequate parking.

Yet Miracle Mile persisted, in part as a tourist hub. In the early 1960s, it became the location of the Los Angeles County Museum of Art (LACMA). The county had a museum, located in Exposition Park south of downtown. Housed in a Beaux-Arts building designed in 1913, it was known as the Los Angeles County Museum of History, Science and Art. In 1959, in recognition that Los Angeles was a major urban center in need of major cultural facilities, the county board of supervisors passed a resolution that authorized the design of a new museum to be devoted to art, remaking the site in Exposition Park into a natural sciences museum. The cost of construction for the new art museum was raised from private contributors. The museum campus, located in Hancock Park at 5905 Wilshire Boulevard, was originally designed by William L. Pereira Associates. In 1977, the George C. Page Museum of La Brea Discoveries, designed by Thornton, Fagan and Associates, opened in Hancock Park to the east of LACMA. Farmer's Market, which went through some economic decline in the 1970s, also retained its tourist appeal, becoming a nostalgic destination, particularly for elderly Jewish tourists.

Miracle Mile and its immediate environs retained their medium commercial and low residential densities despite a continuing flow of proposals for more compact redevelopment. In 1963, sensing an opportunity for a site opposite the future campus of LACMA, A.W. Ross, who was in his eighties, began planning for yet another mixed-use development, to be located on the south side of Wilshire Boulevard between Spaulding Avenue to the east and Ogden Drive to the west. Preliminary designs by the architects Irving D. Shapiro and Sidney Eisenshtat for the $15 million, two-block Wilshire Square proposal were to include at least one office building and two high-rise apartment complexes of twenty-two to twenty-eight stories in height, to include 460 apartments and some retail. This was one of several of Ross's plans for high-rise apartment buildings with commercial spaces along Wilshire Boulevard. Their residents, Ross predicted, would have little reason to leave this area for their everyday needs. In a reversal to his early ideas, which led to the development of Miracle Mile as a car destination, Ross also conceived of a day when residents would have limited need for personal transportation.

By the late 1960s, part of this proposal was abandoned, possibly because of Ross's death in 1968. Located on this site is a tall office building designed by William L. Pereira Associates in 1969, bearing for many years the Variety logo. In another example of redevelopment to pump more fuel into the Miracle Mile–area economy, in the 1980s CBS and A.F. Gilmore Co. proposed building a business and entertainment complex that would have potentially taken up fifty-two acres of land and would have been twice as large as Universal City, Los Angeles's largest entertainment district. The plan included expanded studio space for CBS, the construction of a hotel, theaters, restaurants, shops and offices. At that time, city officials and neighborhood associations voiced concern over the scope of the development, which would have potentially demolished the Farmer's Market, popular with tourists, and the historic Gilmore adobe. The project did not go through.

Playing a part in the conflict over the size of this and other proposed developments was also the question of density near the stations of the planned subway system. One such station was to be located near the intersection of Beverly Boulevard and Fairfax Avenue, adjoining the CBS Television City. While some landowners looked favorably on more dense development proposals, many residential communities did not, and that included the elderly and immigrants living in this area.

PUBLIC TRANSPORTATION

Transportation issues have played an important part in the history of Miracle Mile since its inception, which was predicated on the ubiquity of car ownership. Thus, in the 1930s, public transportation into Miracle Mile was fairly limited. The Pacific Electric red cars ran to the intersection of Pico and San Vicente Boulevards, over a mile to the southeast. The "R" streetcar from downtown stopped near La Brea and Third Street. Wilshire Boulevard was served by yellow and red double-decker buses. Thanks to the popularity of Miracle Mile, traffic congestion quickly became a major issue for residents and for city planners. In the 1950s, city council authorized traffic islands and left turn lanes in an attempt to ensure that traffic moved more smoothly through Miracle Mile. Curb parking along Wilshire Boulevard was removed, and parking meters were installed on side streets. The business community along Miracle Mile was galvanized by A.W. Ross to support these measures. Miracle Mile was included in a variety of plans, some futuristic and some practical, to move city traffic along—plans that were not always perceived as benefitting the district or its environs.

For example, in the early 1960s, there were discussions to build a forty-three-mile-long network of raised monorails in various areas of Los Angeles, including one spanning Wilshire Boulevard. This idea was opposed by the homeowners' associations. Another plan that also did not materialize, but which would have impacted this area, was the 1970s proposal to construct the Beverly Hills Freeway to connect the Hollywood Freeway (the 101) with the San Diego Freeway (the 405), in rough alignment with Melrose Avenue. Public buses have served Miracle Mile and its environs since the 1940s. Metro, the county transportation agency, currently operates local and rapid busses on Wilshire Boulevard (numbers 20 and 720), La Brea Avenue (numbers 212 and 312) and Fairfax Avenue (numbers 217 and 780) and on the major thoroughfares running parallel to Wilshire, such as Third Street (numbers 16 and 316), Beverly Boulevard (number 14) and Olympic Boulevard (numbers 28 and 728). The Los Angeles Department of Transportation operates the DASH shuttle bus services around Fairfax Avenue, just north of Miracle Mile.

In the annals of public transportation, it is the development of the subway system that makes Miracle Mile an illustrative example of late twentieth-century urban planning in Los Angeles. By the 1950s, many corporations moved their headquarters from downtown to the suburbs. This put them closer to the many residential tracts that grew exponentially after World War II. The euphoria of dispersal, however, was relatively short-lived. By the early 1960s, it was clear that the city needed to address street congestion. The energy crisis of the mid-1970s also played a role in driving transportation-related discussions. In addition, the Community Redevelopment Act encouraged making underpriced land in downtown attractive to developers and to corporations to invest in the growth of a unified commercial hub that could bring together thousands of employees, banks, law firms and foreign investment. In other words, there was a growing interest in a revitalized downtown.

While an argument was made that a growing downtown would result in tremendous traffic problems in a city already noted for snared traffic, backers of a centralized downtown supported the development of a subway network as an answer to traffic congestion. The building of a subway was also seen as an opportunity to spur commercial and residential densification of the city, with the assumption that it would increase the value of lands adjacent to subway routes. Along the ailing Miracle Mile, large businesses, such as May Company, also supported the subway with its promised commercial revitalization. While in 1968 the bond issue to implement a rapid-transit system was defeated by voters, the city continued to make plans, seeing the problem of traffic circulation as a priority to be solved. The first phase of the rapid-transit master plan included the Wilshire Corridor route that, by the 1980s, was supposed to connect Fairfax Avenue with downtown. The subway's proposed route was from Seventh Street east of the Harbor Freeway, going westward to Hoover Boulevard and aligning with Wilshire Boulevard at Vermont Avenue. Stations were planned on Miracle Mile at La Brea, Dunsmuir, Masselin and Fairfax Avenues. These stations were closely spaced, in order to provide transit services within walking distance for those living or working within a quarter-mile radius.

In the 1980s, the Southern California Rapid Transit District (RTD) sought $336 million for an eighteen-mile rail stretching from downtown Los Angeles through the Wilshire corridor and into the San Fernando Valley. President Reagan signed legislation providing $100 million in funding. The state assembly began considering raising local money to supplement federal funds. The state legislature passed a law allowing the RTD to create "benefit assessment districts" around the planned subway stations in 1983. Accordingly, property owners would be assessed a tax to pay for the benefits received from owning property near a subway stop. Because federal funding was much less than originally hoped for, RTD planned for bigger developments around subway stations in order to produce more tax dollars for the local share of Metro Rail financing. As expected, large transit-oriented developments did not sit well with some of the local property owners. Yet reading the history of subway development along Wilshire Boulevard solely as a function of real estate interests is overly simplistic.

Emblematic of Los Angeles, planning for rail transit in the Miracle Mile area was entrenched in the mindset of mid-twentieth-century urban growth that defined the city in terms of dispersed suburbanization. For example, while discussing Metro Rail, Councilman Zev Yaroslavsky stated in 1980 that while he wanted mass transit for his Fairfax district, which also included Miracle Mile, he was determined to preserve the neighborhoods' relatively low densities. In public, the political discussions were about protecting the existing built environment by having mass transit without the masses or the massing. The proposed subway stop at the corner of Spaulding Avenue and Wilshire Boulevard included a bus depot and a parking lot. Residents immediately to the south objected, claiming that it would threaten the area's historic and cultural heritage. Particular concern was expressed at the plan to demolish the Craft and Folk Art Museum, located on Wilshire Boulevard, for the parking lot. Members of the Miracle Mile Residential Association agreed that the subway might play an important role in the revitalization of the area and suggested that the stop be relocated to the intersection of Fairfax Avenue and Wilshire Boulevard.

Concern for the architectural and cultural heritage of Miracle Mile was shared by the Los Angeles Conservancy, as can be seen from the statement by the conservancy's executive director that appeared in the *Los Angeles Times*: "The existing framework of buildings is important to the definition of the streetscape and street corridor of this historic boulevard. Its interruption for a surface parking lot, a heavily intensive land use in terms of land consumption, seems a poor land-use decision for Wilshire Boulevard." This unease over a proposal to build a parking lot on a stretch of Wilshire that in the 1920s and 1930s touted access by car points to considerable changes in the built environment and in the urban sensibility of the residents that occurred in the span of half a century.

Some of the transit-related developments were simply very large. A particular example was the proposal for the redevelopment of the east side of Fairfax Avenue between Wilshire Boulevard and Third Street, to occur in tandem with plans for a subway stop. Included in these plans was the relocation of the May Company store from Fairfax and Wilshire northward, to a location near Fairfax and Sixth Street, in order to make way for several tall hotel buildings. The plans called for the construction of office high-rise buildings around the relocated May Company, a "new, stepped-up configuration of apartments" supplanting the low-rise garden apartments of Parklabrea, as well as a shopping mall and a series of parking structures interconnected via a people-mover system.

Also problematic for Metro Rail construction was the existence of the La Brea Tar Pits. Because of the large tar reserves, particularly between Curson and Fairfax Avenues, paleontologists warned that fossil bones could be found anywhere in the area and would require proper excavation, storage and curation. A proposed subway route was to pass through the oil fields near Third Street and Ogden Drive. In 1985, there was a fiery methane gas explosion at 6200 Third Street, underneath a Ross Dress for Less store, which resulted in injuries to several dozen people. The methane explosion put an end to discussions on transportation-related developments here, which also included a proposed subway station at Beverly Boulevard and Fairfax Avenue.

In the 1990s, Miracle Mile's economic conditions began to improve. The commercial areas around it expanded with the building of the open-air Grove shopping mall, located where a grove of trees used to stand. Additional multistory (although not high-rise) buildings with apartments and condominiums were constructed along Third Street, Sixth Street and Wilshire Boulevard. The LACMA campus expanded to include the historic May Company building and several newly designed structures. Currently, Los Angeles has several subway lines operating. The Purple Line runs from downtown to the intersection of Wilshire Boulevard and Western Avenue, several miles east of Miracle Mile. The passage of Measure R in 2008 allowed for partial funding for the westward extension of the Purple Line. Approved stations for Miracle Mile are planned for La Brea and Fairfax Avenues, the latter highly supported by LACMA, which sees it as improving access to the museum.

These post–World War II discussions about the fate and shape of the subway system were not without irony. The Mile was the first shopping area of Los Angeles not built near trolley tracks and the first to provide off-site parking. It was symbolic of the displacement of downtown Los Angeles as a commercial hub and spelled an end to the reach of the electric streetcars. Miracle Mile was also a microcosm in the advancement of architectural ideas. In its early days, companies such as Desmond's financed the buildings into which they moved. This became less of a practice after World War II, particularly on the stretch of Wilshire between La Brea Avenue and Hauser Boulevard, which was considerably built up.

As Miracle Mile's fortunes changed, so did its architecture. Some of the Mile's iconic buildings designed in the architectural idioms prevalent in the early and middle parts of the twentieth century were demolished; others survived. Some have local designation as historic resources. The economic booms and recessions of the late twentieth and early twenty-first centuries are also beginning to leave their mark on the Mile's built landscape. Some of the parking lots disappeared, and the expansion of the subway system will bring additional architectural changes. Miracle Mile and its environs are now a mixture of commercial buildings, single-family residential neighborhoods and multifamily residential complexes. It is also home to a variety of cultural institutions. The next chapter is a checklist, albeit incomplete, of the architectural and public art historic legacies of Wilshire Boulevard on Miracle Mile.

Chapter 4

WALKING THE MILE

This chapter lists historic locations and buildings, either extant or demolished, on Wilshire Boulevard in Miracle Mile. It starts near Mansfield Avenue, moving west toward Fairfax Avenue. Given the complexity of the Mile's history, this checklist is by no means exhaustive. While by the middle of the twentieth century, Miracle Mile was densely developed between La Brea and Hauser, it had a considerable number of vacant and parking lots west of Hauser, particularly on the south side of Wilshire. Currently, Miracle Mile retains some of the original buildings from the 1930s, although a number of structures from before World War II were demolished. Miracle Mile also has significant Modernist buildings constructed from the late 1940s into the 1960s. Some of the postwar buildings were demolished relatively recently. There are also a number of commercial structures from the 1970s and 1980s. The remaking and rebuilding of Miracle Mile continues in the early twenty-first century, particularly east of La Brea Avenue and around Hauser Boulevard. In the 1980s, the Los Angeles Conservancy launched an effort to designate Miracle Mile as a historic district, based on the existence of nineteen pre–World War II buildings considered contributors to the Mile's period of historical significance. This chapter moves east to west between major intersections. Odd-numbered addresses are on the north side of Wilshire Boulevard; even-numbered addresses are on the south side.

MANSFIELD AVENUE TO HAUSER BOULEVARD, NORTH SIDE

5055 Wilshire Boulevard

The Carnation Company headquarters were located here in a nine-story building of reinforced concrete, which was designed by Stiles and Robert Clements and erected by the William Simpson Company in 1949. It reportedly cost over $1.5 million to build. The building's exterior was white, with the ground floor faced

The Carnation Company headquarters building, photographed in 1949. *Courtesy of the* Examiner.

in red granite. There was a three-story structure atop the ninth floor, which contained ventilating equipment and bore the company's logo. The interior had soft pastel colors, perhaps in contrast to the rectilinear Modernist exterior. A two-story adjacent structure contained an employee training area and a coffee shop. Carnation moved its headquarters out of this building around 1988. Barker Pacific Group (BPG) acquired it in 1990. The building was gutted to its poured-concrete frame, and the coffee shop was demolished. The current structure is twice the size of the original and has an Art Deco–style exterior.

5151 Wilshire Boulevard

In 1954, Stiles and Robert Clements designed a Modernist building for the Cadillac Motor Car Division. The two-story, flat-roofed structure was L shaped in plan and had large glass windows on three sides of the first story. It had an overhanging steel canopy, above which rose an unadorned second story that featured the dealership sign. From about 1965 until its demolition in 2008, this was the location of Lou Ehlers Cadillac.

5209 Wilshire Boulevard

The Deco Building, designed in 1929 by Morgan, Walls and Clements, is located west of the intersection with Sycamore Avenue. It was constructed for the Security First National Bank for about $85,000. The building's distinctive

This 1926 photograph shows the Spanish Revival–style commercial block that was located on the north side of Wilshire Boulevard, just west of Sycamore Avenue. Located on this site is the Deco Building. *Courtesy of "Dick" Whittington.*

Zigzag Moderne exterior is clad in black and gold terra cotta, designed by Rufus Keeler, and its tall windows are partially shaded by ornamental metal cutwork. The building was designated Los Angeles Historic Cultural Monument #813 in 2005. In the 1920s, there stood on this site a low-rise Spanish Revival–style commercial building that already housed a branch of Security First National, as well as various other businesses. What remained of this commercial block was demolished in the 1980s. Its site is currently occupied by a Jack-in-the-Box eatery.

5213-5231 Wilshire Boulevard. Northeast Corner with La Brea Avenue

In the late 1920s, one of Gilmore Company's gasoline stations was located on this corner. To the east of it, there was a small stucco building with a hipped roof that housed a Wimpy Grills eatery. In 1930, the businessman E. Clem Wilson financed the construction of a commercial Art Deco building, designed by Mendel Meyer and Phillip Holler, at a cost of $1.5 million. The building's plan was in the form of a Greek cross. Utilities, such as elevators, stairways and plumbing, were placed in the center. Its parking lot was located to the northeast, on the corner of Sycamore Avenue and Carling Way. The building is notable for its massive tower, the rhythmic effect of its vertical lines and the setbacks at different levels to allow outdoor and roofing space for many of the offices. A revolving beacon, which originally served as a guide for aircraft, was a distinctive feature for several decades until 1984. That year, the building's owner since 1961, Mutual of Omaha, had it removed during renovation. The building's storefronts and entrance were modernized in 1955 under the supervision of Welton Becket and Associates.

5301 Wilshire Boulevard. Northwest Corner with La Brea Avenue

A Spanish-style commercial building designed by the architects George Elmore Gable and C. Stanley Wyant was erected here in 1928 to house the Dyas-Carlton Café. Parking was in the back. The restaurant's large interior, which could seat about 250 people, had an arched Churrigueresque-style ceiling and wide windows. By the early 1930s, it became known as just Carlton's, and in the late 1930s, the building housed McDonnell's Café. In 1949, this location became the site of Tilford's Restaurant and lounge,

Aluminum modules by Jim Isermann decorate the Metro Agency regional building on the northwest corner of Wilshire Boulevard and La Brea Avenue. Photographed in 2010. *Courtesy of Ruth Wallach.*

designed by Welton Becket and Associates. The Southern California Rapid Transit District purchased the lot in 1984 for its Metro Rail subway project. The small business structure, which was located to the immediate west, was demolished in the 1980s for a parking lot. The corner building was remodeled and has served as Metro Agency's regional customer service office since 1987. In 2006, its exterior was wrapped in a sculptural work designed by the artist Jim Isermann, made of five hundred aluminum modules.

5353–5359 Wilshire Boulevard, Northwest Corner with Detroit Street

A building housing Melody Lane Café, designed by Marcus P. Miller and constructed by Baruch Company, opened on this corner in 1937. It had colored terra cotta veneer on the exterior and a dining room that had murals by Anthony Heinsbergen. A branch of California Bank opened in a new building designed by Earl Heitschmidt and Whiting S. Thompson at this

Drawing of California Bank designed by Earl Heitschmidt and Whiting S. Thompson in 1953. The building was located on the northwest corner of Wilshire Boulevard and Detroit Street. *Courtesy of the* Examiner.

location in 1954. Its exterior was of light tan-colored travertine marble, with a glass entrance faced in black granite. Over the years, this commercial building leased spaces to cafés, travel agencies and Hahn's Music store, which sold pianos and organs. The current multistory apartment building called Museum Gardens, with commercial spaces on the first floor, was erected in 2006. Elements of the original ground-floor façade from the 1930s are still visible on the block.

5379 Wilshire Boulevard, Northeast Corner with Cloverdale Avenue

This commercial block was constructed in 1928 for the Cline & Cline Company, a noted sporting goods company, which was wooed to open on Miracle Mile by A.W. Ross. By 1931, the company was bought out by Olympic Sporting Goods, and this location was renamed. In the early 1940s, A. Stern and Sons opened a fur shop that remained here for several decades. Over the years, boutiques and beauty salons leased storefronts on this block. The 1936 reinforced concrete building at 5401–5405 Wilshire Boulevard, on the northwest corner with Cloverdale Avenue, was designed in a Streamline Moderne style by Alvah Edward Norstrom and Milton L. Anderson for Sontag's Drugstore. Sontag's advertised a complete fountain grill that could seat one hundred people and an interior with controlled temperature, still a novelty. Over the years, the premises were occupied by a variety of shops and restaurants. The building currently houses Wilshire Beauty Supply.

5413-5425 Wilshire Boulevard, between Cloverdale and Cochran Avenues

In March 1935, the Atlantic and Pacific Tea Company (A&P) opened its "Food Palace" on this block, in a reinforced concrete structure that cost $35,000 to erect. The interior had arched trusses that spanned eighty feet, allowing for natural light and an airy interior unobstructed by support columns. When it opened, the A&P advertised an adjoining parking lot for five hundred cars and a location within convenient driving distance from the residential districts of Hollywood, Westwood, Beverly Hills, Cheviot Hills, Culver City and Westlake (now MacArthur Park). The building later came to house several food markets. Brown's Bakery was located at 5423 Wilshire. In the 1930s, Wimpy Grills hamburger eatery, which later became the Flying Saucer, was located on the northeast corner of Wilshire and Cochran. The flying saucer–shaped design of the 1990s façade of the Staples office supply store, currently located here, pays homage to these eateries, although both Wimpy Grills and the Flying Saucer were housed in a one-story square stucco building with a hipped roof.

This block on the northeast corner of Wilshire Boulevard and Cochran Avenue housed Wimpy Grills, which later became the Flying Saucer restaurant, as well as Brown's Bakery and a food market, as seen in this 1960s photograph. *Courtesy of the* Examiner.

5455 Wilshire Boulevard, Northwest Corner with Cochran Avenue

The Modernist twenty-one-story, 280-foot-high Lee Tower, built in 1959, was a project of W. Douglas Lee and D. Everett Lee, a father-son team. It was among the first skyscrapers built in Los Angeles after the height limit

View of Lee Tower, photographed in 2012. In the foreground is the 1930s building that houses Wilshire Beauty Supply store. Beyond it may be seen the 1990s Staples office supply store, shaped like a flying saucer. *Courtesy of Ruth Wallach.*

This photograph from around 1960 shows the Streamline Moderne storefront of the men's clothing store Zachary All, currently occupied by a Walgreens pharmacy. *Courtesy of the* Examiner.

ordinance of 150 feet was relaxed in 1957 and the first such building on Miracle Mile. The building's glass curtain walls hang on a steel frame, and the entire column-like structure sits on top of a six-story garage. The commercial building on the northeast corner with Dunsmuir, at 5467–5475 Wilshire, was built in 1936. White Spot Restaurant operated at 5467 from the 1930s to around 1940. From the 1950s into the 1990s, this was the location of the clothing store Zachary All. The current tenant of this block is a Walgreens pharmacy. The original Streamline Moderne design can still be discerned in the horizontal lines above the awnings.

5501-5505 Wilshire Boulevard, Northwest Corner with Dunsmuir Avenue

This building was designed by Frank Rasche in 1929 for the Seaboard National Bank, which, like many early businesses on Miracle Mile, advertised a parking lot in the back. It cost approximately $75,000 to construct. The architectural style mixed Roman and Egyptian Revival with elements of Zigzag Moderne. The exterior was completed in terra cotta and art stone, while the interior was finished in Italian marble. In 1935, an Armenian restaurant opened on the premises, decorated in the style of "Old Constantinople." Robert Lippert, owner of motion picture theaters, purchased the building in 1959 for about $350,000 for the headquarters of his Electro-Vision Corporation. Since the 1980s, this structure has housed the Korean Cultural Center.

5515-5519 Wilshire Boulevard, between Dunsmuir and Burnside Avenues

The El Rey Theatre was designed about 1936 by Clifford A. Balch in a combination of Zigzag Moderne and Art Deco styles. It is particularly notable for its neon marquee. The El Rey served as a movie theater until the 1980s, first for the Fox and then for the Mann chains, and later as a revival house. In the 1980s, the building housed a dance club, called Wall Street, to the great consternation of the residential neighborhoods nearby, and in the early 1990s, it had a Russian restaurant and nightclub. In 1991, the El Rey Theatre was designated Los Angeles Historic Cultural Monument #520, and its auditorium is currently used for music venues. Located at

View of the building originally constructed for Bank of America in 1954, located on the northeast corner of Wilshire Boulevard and Burnside Avenue. The marquee of the El Rey Theatre is seen to the right. Photographed in 2012. *Courtesy of Ruth Wallach.*

5525 Wilshire Boulevard, on the northeast corner with Burnside Avenue, is a three-story Modernist building constructed by George Novikoff for the developer Herbert Kronish in 1954. The first tenant was a branch of Bank of America. The building served many commercial establishments over the years and is currently home to a hair goods company.

5555 Wilshire Boulevard. Northwest Corner with Burnside Avenue

Ontra Cafeteria was located here from 1947, when the building was constructed, until the mid-1970s. The building's façade was considerably redesigned and currently houses a branch of Smart and Final. In 1956, Bond's Clothing moved into a building designed by Stiles O. Clements at 5575 Wilshire Boulevard, on the northeast corner with Ridgeley Drive. It was erected on a block previously occupied by a parking lot. A striking feature of the building was an exterior mosaic glass wall made of multicolored glass

A 1956 drawing of Bond's Clothing designed by Stiles O. Clements for the northeast corner with Ridgeley Drive. *Courtesy of the* Examiner.

imported from Venice. A parking lot was built behind the store at the same time. The interior was designed by Eugene Burke, Charles M. Kober and Harold J. Nicolais. After Bond's closed, Adray's Discount Store moved here in 1981. Currently, this location is occupied by a Rite-Aid pharmacy.

5601 Wilshire Boulevard, Northwest Corner with Ridgeley Drive

In the early 1930s, a two-story Spanish Revival–style commercial building was erected by Ben Meyerson. From the mid-1950s to the mid-1960s, a branch of Dupar's Restaurant operated here. Ralphs Grocery Company bought the site on the northeast corner with Hauser, at 5627–5631 Wilshire, in 1924 and opened a store, its twelfth, on September 19, 1928. It was designed by Stiles O. Clements as a Spanish-style arcade clad in gray granite. The interior had two large domed ceilings with wooden beams. Arabesque-like ornamentation decorated the spaces between the beams. The interior also featured a mezzanine with stalls for merchandise. Smaller businesses filled the rest of the arcade. This Ralphs was one of the earliest stores to offer a large variety of groceries combined with self-service. To quote from the *Los Angeles Times*, the shopper "may order her coffee, and while it is being ground, may pick out herself the other articles she wishes, and, assembling these without waiting for attention from hurried salesfolk, may immediately pay her bill and receive her merchandise." The buildings were demolished in the 1980s. The entire block between Ridgeley and Hauser is currently occupied by a large Ralphs supermarket which was constructed in 1994.

Mansfield Avenue to Hauser Boulevard, South Side

5112 Wilshire Boulevard, between Orange Drive and Mansfield Avenue

This Art Deco building was designed by Walker & Eisen with Clifford A. Balch, circa 1932. It was a United Artists movie theater and eventually became known as the Four Star. The building operated as a movie theater into the 1990s. In 2001, it became a Christian center. In 2007, it was renamed Oasis Theatre, continuing to offer church services on Sundays. The five-story commercial

The Oasis Theatre building, photographed in 2012. *Courtesy of Ruth Wallach.*

The West Coast Ritz Theatre building is seen in this photograph shortly after it was built in 1926. *Courtesy of "Dick" Whittington.*

building located across it on the southwest corner with Orange Drive, at 5150 Wilshire Boulevard, was constructed circa 1957 on an undeveloped lot. Another theater, the Fox Ritz Theatre, designed by Lewis A. Smith in a Spanish Colonial Revival style, opened at 5214 Wilshire, on the southwest corner with Sycamore Avenue, in 1926. For many years, it was operated by Fox West Coast Theatres. For a while in the 1960s, the building was home to the Lindy Opera Company. The building was demolished in 1977 for a surface parking lot.

5220 Wilshire Boulevard, Southeast Corner with La Brea Avenue

A two-story building block that extended south along La Brea Avenue and east along Wilshire was built for Pardee Drugstore in the late 1920s. For a while, the Bank of Italy (later Bank of America) leased offices in this building until it moved across La Brea to a new building constructed on the southwest corner with Wilshire Boulevard. The Pardee Drugstore building remained here until the early 1960s. In 1964, Columbia Savings and Loan Association built its headquarters on this site. The thirty-eight-thousand-square-foot office building was designed by Irving D. Shapiro and Associates at a cost of $1.5 million. It was to be the first phase of a high-rise office complex that was planned for the site. The company wanted the structural elements to "dominate the design, giving an air of stature, solidity, strength and soundness." The concrete and glass structure was suspended from four concrete piers, each purportedly weighing 375 tons, mounted on a platform.

This design, according to the architect, evoked the style of public buildings of ancient Greece. Its first floor had a glass exterior, and its upper stories were ensconced in sculptured concrete that projected beyond the glass, thus serving as sunshade for the stories below. Next to the building on the Wilshire and La Brea sides stood two eighty-five-foot-tall pylons that held commercial signage. A notable feature of the building was a stained-glass interior skylight, designed by Roger Darricarrere, which capped a light-well shaft that extended from the main floor to the roof. A sculptural fountain designed by the artist Taki in the shape of a metal screen rested in a shallow pool facing La Brea Avenue. The building's concrete brutalism and Modernist unornamented symmetrical forms were considered emblematic

Sculpture by Taki, installed in 1965 on the La Brea Avenue side of the Columbia Savings and Loan Association building. Photographed in 2010, before the building was demolished. *Courtesy of Ruth Wallach.*

of post–World War II banking architecture. After Columbia Savings and Loan moved out, the building was used by a variety of banking institutions, and in 1994 it was acquired by what eventually became the Wilshire Grace Church. The church sold it in 2005, and the building was demolished in 2010. As of the writing of this book, the entire block is under construction for a mixed-use retail structure with 480 apartment units.

5308-5310 Wilshire Boulevard, Southwest Corner with La Brea Avenue

In 1925 Bank of Italy (later Bank of America) purchased a lot on this corner and financed a commercial building. The retailer Brooks Clothing and a variety of small shops leased spaces. The current building housing a branch of Bank of America was constructed in 1942. The commercial building at 5328 Wilshire, on the southeast corner with Detroit Street, was constructed in 1936. It was designed in the Spanish Colonial Revival style. The original façade was retained into the early 1980s.

5350-5352 Wilshire Boulevard, Southwest Corner with Detroit Street

This building was constructed in 1937 for S.H. Kress Company, which opened a store here in early 1938. The company advertised this location as being of modern design, with high ceilings, spacious isles to make shopping easy and a modern system of lighting flooding the store

Leed's Shoes opened in a redesigned building on the southeast corner of Wilshire Boulevard and Cloverdale Avenue in early September 1949. The building's current façade has been considerably altered. *Courtesy of the* Examiner.

with light at all hours. Meghrig Coin and Stamp Supply Company has been at this location for several decades. Currently, the ground floor is occupied by a U.S. Post Office station. The commercial block between Detroit Street and Cloverdale Avenue, at 5362–5376 Wilshire Boulevard, was initially constructed in the late 1920s into the early 1930s. Its most notable feature is the façade of the Darkroom designed by Marcus P. Miller in 1937 for a photography store that stayed at this location for decades. Designated Los Angeles Historic Cultural Monument #451 in 1989, it resembles a 35mm camera and currently houses a sports bar. The building at 5376, on the southeast corner with Cloverdale, was redesigned in a Streamline Moderne style in 1949 for Leed's Shoes. The décor was done in pastels and natural wood colors. Very little of the original façade remains. The building now houses a hair salon.

5400-5420 Wilshire Boulevard, Entire Block between Cloverdale and Cochran Avenues

The Dominguez building was designed in 1930 by Morgan, Walls & Clements. The apparel firm Myer Siegel & Company leased floor space on the first and second stories, making it the company's largest branch. Myer Siegel was attracted to this location by calculating that 435,000 people resided within a short distance, wielding a purchasing power of more than $600 million a year. The store opened on October 26, 1931. It had a canopied entrance framed in glass and metal and a second, private entrance in the rear. The firm of Joseph L. Feil and Bernard R. Paradise was engaged to do the interior design, which featured inlaid floors and décor done in tones of beige, blue and green, accented by maple wood. Later in the 1930s, the apparel store Wetherby Kayser and the women's shoe store C.H. Baker also moved into the business block formed by the Dominguez building. In January 1958, Dr. John Martin Hiss purchased the Dominguez building in excess of $1 million and moved the headquarters of his Hiss Foot Clinic to this location. For a while, the Dominguez building was also known as Hiss Tower.

5450-5454 Wilshire Boulevard, Southwest Corner with Cochran Avenue

In 1936, A.W. Ross announced that the Brooks Clothing Company would move its branch from the southwest corner of Wilshire Boulevard and La

Brea Avenue to a new structure designed by the architects Morgan, Walls & Clements and that several other businesses would relocate to this address, as well. Harris & Frank, another clothing company, merged with Brooks Clothing in 1947 and opened a Harris & Frank at this location. In 1952, Harris & Frank contracted with the architect Stiles O. Clements to modernize the store. Clements's modern redesign used Roman brick, aluminum trim, glass and concrete. The interior was redecorated by Maurice H. Fleishman. By the 1980s, Harris & Frank had a clearance outlet located at 5570 Wilshire Boulevard, between Ridgeley Drive and Burnside Avenue, and in 1989 the retailer was gone from Miracle Mile.

5478-5482 Wilshire Boulevard, Southeast Corner with Dunsmuir Avenue

This is one of the earliest commercial structures on Miracle Mile, built in 1927–28 and designed in a Spanish Colonial Revival style by Frank M. Tyler. In the 1930s, various retailers, including a Woolworth's, were located on this block. Mandel's Shoe store occupied the corner closest to Dunsmuir into the late 1970s. The interior of Mandel's was remodeled in 1949 by Eugene Burke and Charles M. Kober in what was called an ultra-modern California style featuring soft color contrasts. Over the years, there have been many other businesses on this block, including, in the 1990s, a Georgian-Russian restaurant. Current tenants include an Indian restaurant and various other businesses.

5514 Wilshire Boulevard, Entire Block between Dunsmuir and Burnside Avenues

Wilshire Tower was the first major structure built on Miracle Mile. Designed by Gilbert Stanley Underwood in 1929, it combines Streamline Moderne Zigzag and Art Deco styles. Its nine-story tower has curved corners and Egyptian-motif carvings. Ross used the Wilshire Tower building to lure Desmond's, at that time the largest men's clothing store in downtown Los Angeles, to open a branch here in March 1929. The building was designed to have front and rear display windows and entrances, with a parking lot in the rear, so that shoppers would have immediate access from their cars to the individual stores on the block. The presence of Desmond's on Miracle Mile lured other stores and business establishments.

Desmond's and Silverwood's store signs still grace the top of Wilshire Tower. Photographed in 2013. *Courtesy of Ruth Wallach.*

In September 1929, Silverwood's, with interior designed by Joseph L. Feil and Bernard R. Paradise, opened right next door, in the two-story west wing adjoining the tower. On opening day, the Wilshire Silverwood's entertained revelers with acrobatic shows that included clowns and horses. Like Desmond's, Silverwood's offered plenty of parking to the south. At that time, the president of the company, G.E. Nagel, predicted that by 1934 Wilshire boulevard would be comparable to Fifth Avenue in New York; Michigan Boulevard in Chicago; Pennsylvania Avenue in Washington, D.C.; and Rue de la Paix in Paris—all locations for fine shops. Desmond's closed this branch in 1980, and Silverwood's closed in 1985. The Desmond's and Silverwood's neon signs remain to this day at the top of the tower. On December 8, 1987, after negotiations between the local homeowners working with the Los Angeles Conservancy and the owner of the building who initially wanted to demolish it, Wilshire Tower was designated Los Angeles Historic Cultural Monument #332, the first major structure in Miracle Mile to receive the designation. Currently, the building houses the Ace Gallery.

5550-5570 Wilshire Boulevard,
Entire Block between Burnside Avenue and Ridgeley Drive

In 1936, the architecture firm Morgan, Walls & Clements designed a two-story store for the men's apparel Phelps-Terkel on the southwest corner with Burnside Avenue. This location was attractive to the retailer because it was close to the Wilshire Tower and its successful retail anchor, Desmond's. In 1944, the apparel firm Mullen & Bluett had the entire block designed into a two-story store by Stiles O. Clements at a reported cost of $2 million. It opened in February 1949. The interior and fixtures were designed by Eugene Burke and Charles M. Kober. This location advertised itself as serving clients not just in the Miracle Mile area but also in Hollywood and Westwood. The store's interior featured a mural depicting the firm's first store, which opened in 1883 in downtown Los Angeles. Mullen & Bluett closed the Wilshire store in April 1972. Phelps-Terkel remained in its location until 1976. Coldwell Bank had offices on the premises in the 1980s. Currently, the block is occupied by a large apartment building constructed in the late 2000s and designed in a Streamline Moderne style.

Seen in this drawing is the Mullen & Bluett store designed by Stiles O. Clements for Miracle Mile in 1949. *Courtesy of the* Examiner.

5600 Wilshire Boulevard. Southeast Corner with Hauser Boulevard

This was the site of Coulter's department store. B.F. Coulter opened his dry goods store in downtown Los Angeles in 1878. Over the years, it grew into a department store and moved to several locations in downtown. In 1938, A.W. Ross lured Coulter's to Miracle Mile, into a six-story Streamline Moderne building designed by Stiles O. Clements for the store. In the 1950s, Coulter's went through a renovation and added a second parking lot on the northwest corner of Hauser Boulevard and Eighth Street. In the 1970s, the location became a Broadway department store. The building was demolished in 1980, at which time a mixed-use development combining office and retail space with residential condominiums was planned. The proposed plan, designed by Albert C. Martin and Associates to span several blocks of Wilshire, from Ridgeley Drive on the east to Masselin Avenue on the west, was to be called Intercontinental Centre. It was seen as an important development to revitalize the slumping economic fortunes of Miracle Mile.

This photograph shows the elegant interior of the fur shop at Coulter's on Miracle Mile, after the store was renovated in 1954. *Courtesy of the* Examiner.

In the 1980s, Western Continental Investment, which was variously identified as based in Hong Kong and Malaysia, planned a twenty-two-story, 328-room hotel and an office building here. The initial design was by William L. Pereira Associates. This project met with considerable opposition from local residents. The site remained vacant until the middle of the first decade of the twenty-first century, when a five-story, mixed-use apartment building was constructed.

HAUSER BOULEVARD TO FAIRFAX AVENUE, NORTH SIDE

5651-5657 Wilshire Boulevard, Northwest Corner with Hauser Boulevard

A commercial block with several buildings appears to have opened in 1931, with the building on the corner designed by Carl Lindbom. The block's earliest tenants were Western Auto Supply Company, an automobile supplies store, and for several years, a photography studio that doubled as an exhibition space. It was used for a long-term exhibition that showed designs by Carl Lindbom and his associate, William Tuntke, promoting what the two referred to as "international architecture." For many years in the latter part of the twentieth century, the Lindbom-designed building had a Chinese restaurant called Shanghai Winter

The Marfay building, located at 5657 Wilshire Boulevard and designed in 1949 by Welton Becket, is seen in this 1955 photograph by Julius Shulman. © *J. Paul Getty Trust. Used with permission. Julius Shulman Photography Archive, Research Library at the Getty Research Institute (2004.R.10).*

Garden. As of the writing of this book, it houses an International House of Pancakes (IHOP). The five-story building immediately to the west, at number 5657, was designed in 1949 by Welton Becket and Walter Wurdeman for the Marfay Development Company. The jewelers Donavan & Seamans and a branch of Foreman and Clark's clothing store were located here at various times. Welton Becket and Associates had its offices on the top floor, and in the 1950s, there were art exhibitions held in the building. The façade was considerably altered in the ensuing decades.

5665 Wilshire Boulevard. Northeast Corner with Masselin Avenue

In 1934, Kalman Loeb Sr. opened the Wilshire Bowl, a popular restaurant and music club, in a one-story Streamline Moderne building that was located on this corner. The building's most notable feature was a tower that faced Masselin Avenue. A decade later, circa 1943–47, another restaurant and club, called Slapsy Maxie's, was located here. The building was demolished around 1949. In March 1951, Van de Kamp's Bakeries opened a coffee shop at this location, designed by Welton Becket and Associates. This was the company's largest restaurant on the West Coast, containing twenty-

This architect's drawing shows Van de Kamp's restaurant and bakery, designed by Welton Becket in 1951. Behind is the Marfay Building, also designed by Becket. *Courtesy of the* Examiner.

one thousand square feet of space. It included a parking facility for three hundred cars. The counter had eighty-five seats, and there was a sidewalk café separated from Wilshire Boulevard by a glass wall. By the 1970s, this location had a store selling Chinese and oriental-style furniture. The current building front for Office Depot dates to 2005.

5757 Wilshire Boulevard, Northwest of Masselin Avenue

In early 1947, the Prudential Insurance Company announced that it planned to establish its western head office in Los Angeles, a very important deal for Miracle Mile. Welton Becket and Walter Wurdeman designed the height-limit building in the style of International Moderne. The site selected for the building encompassed ten acres between Curson and Masselin Avenues on the north side of Wilshire Boulevard, which were owned by the University of Southern California. On March 3, 1948, acting British consul Christopher Kemball presented Prudential with a piece of the Rock of Gibraltar, to be polished, carved and set as a cornerstone for the new building. The Prudential Building cost $7 million to construct. The unadorned exterior was clad in ribbed terra cotta and precast concrete veneer. Control of sunlight was provided by extruded aluminum canopies, or "eyebrows," over the west-facing façade. An important feature was its setback from the sidewalk along Wilshire Boulevard to permit landscaping across the entire front. Such landscaping features became a mainstay of Modernist architecture in Los Angeles and elsewhere.

In late 1955, ground was broken to add a ten-story wing to the north, also designed by Welton Becket and Associates, which cost $2 million. Like the original structure, the new wing had a steel skeleton and reinforced concrete floors. At that time, additional canopies were also added over the southern façade. The Prudential Building was among the earliest to use vermiculite as fireproofing material. The building won architectural and engineering accolades, in part for its use of lightweight aggregates as building materials. It was said that its innovative construction eliminated thirteen thousand tons of dead weight and reduced construction costs by 10 percent. The Prudential Building became a landmark of Miracle Mile, not only because of its architectural design, but also because of the perimeter lighting that highlighted its mass at night. As a concession to some need for decorativeness in a starkly geometric exterior, the first story of the building features state seals cast in bronze that are visible from the sidewalk.

On December 2, 1948, Ohrbach's opened a women's apparel shop in the four-story part of the Prudential complex located on the east side, also designed by Welton Becket and Walter Wurdeman. The *Los Angeles Times* estimated that over twenty thousand women came to the store on opening day. Extra traffic officers were brought in to oversee the intersection of Wilshire Boulevard and Masselin Avenue, as well as other nearby intersections. Traffic on Wilshire Boulevard was reportedly bumper-to-bumper starting at Highland Avenue east of the Miracle Mile district. The design of the store was noted for its fluidity of spaces, a style considered characteristic of Southern California interior architecture. Flow of foot traffic was directed in a circular fashion around clusters of "island" counters, which were surrounded by smaller specialty departments. Floor spaces could be rearranged through the use of portable partitions to meet seasonal needs. The foyer on the Wilshire Boulevard side had a stylized decorative panel of horses and a rider designed by Mary T. Bowling. The children's department on the third floor had a mural by Edward Meshekoff, which depicted animals,

Shoe salon at the Ohrbach's Wilshire store, photographed by Julius Shulman in 1959. © *J. Paul Getty Trust. Used with permission. Julius Shulman Photography Archive, Research Library at the Getty Research Institute (2004.R.10).*

children and cowboys. The store's executive offices were decorated with paintings and photographs, including works by Aaron Bohrod, Joe Jones, Adolf Dehn, Fran Soldini and James Fitzsimmons. In 1969, Ohrbach's relocated out of the Prudential Building to a building previously occupied by Seibu Department store on the southeast corner of Wilshire Boulevard and Fairfax Avenue.

In 1971, Prudential Square, as the complex became known, underwent a $3 million remodeling and expansion by A.C. Martin & Associates. By this time, there were quite a few other tall buildings nearby, and the complex was no longer the dramatic post–World War II architectural feature of Miracle

The 1971 *Primavera* fountain designed by Aristides Demetrios is located in front of Museum Square, formerly Prudential Square. Photographed in 2012. *Courtesy of Ruth Wallach.*

Mile. Part of the remodel was the design of a pedestrian-friendly forecourt on the Wilshire side to emulate a European plaza. To make the forecourt visually interesting to foot and car traffic in this area, a large fountain called *Primavera*, designed by Aristides Demetrios, was installed in 1971. It is a thirty-five-foot tall, U-shaped abstract sculpture made of bronze that some say also resembles a clothespin. Water jets into a small basin that surrounds the sculpture. In July 1982, the complex was acquired by Museum Square Associates, a joint venture between Ogo Associates and the J.H. Snyder Group, and was renamed Museum Square. The architecture firm Maxwell Starckman & Associates renovated the building, with Stephen Barrett Chase doing interior redesign. By this time, Prudential had moved its offices and staff to other locations in Southern California. In 1983, a five-level parking structure was added to the north of the building. In 1985, J.H. Snyder refurbished the old Ohrbach's space into an office building called the Promenade. The Prudential Building currently houses a variety of corporate and entertainment industry offices.

5773 Wilshire Boulevard, Northeast of Curson Avenue

In 1949, the New York Hat store opened in this portion of Prudential Square. Its storefront was designed in the California modern style with a broad entrance trimmed in redwood and cypress. Parking was in the rear. The store remained here until the mid-1950s, after which the site served a variety of businesses, including Kaufman Furs. In the 1970s, an art gallery that was managed by KFAC Radio was also located here. Most of this block was rebuilt in the 1980s. For the past few decades, the tenants at this location have been restaurants and eateries. Its central anchor is the Marie Callender's restaurant, which was designed in 1985 to look like a Victorian building, complete with nineteenth-century-style lamps, wood panels and brass knobs. Inside are a series of murals depicting Wilshire Boulevard in the 1930s and 1940s. The bronze bust of A.W. Ross by Holger and Helen Jensen is located on a traffic island immediately to the west.

5801 and 5905 Wilshire Boulevard, Entire Block between Curson Avenue and Ogden Drive

This part of Miracle Mile contains a park named after George Allan Hancock. The park is noted for its tar deposits, the George C. Page Museum at the La Brea Tar Pits and the Los Angeles County Museum of Art (LACMA). Since 1913, the Los Angeles County Museum of History, Science and Art was located in Exposition Park, south of downtown Los Angeles. Already in the 1930s, there were proposals to build an art museum in Hancock Park, deeded by George Allan Hancock to Los Angeles County, so that the art collection could be housed in its own facility. It was argued that a separate art museum would allow for the display of the existing art works, many of which were kept in storage, and that it would also attract art bequests and funds to grow into a major comprehensive art institution.

In 1958, the museum's board of trustees voted to establish a separate art museum on Wilshire Boulevard. Museum Associates, a nonprofit organization, was tasked with fundraising for the new museum, the construction cost of which was estimated to be over $11 million. The county board of supervisors approved the location for the museum on a portion of Hancock Park. The supervisors also agreed to provide operational funding for the museum. Initial plans recommended tapping Ludwig Mies van der Rohe as architect, to place the new museum on the international architectural and cultural map. Ultimately, the board of trustees appointed William L. Pereira Associates to do the master planning. Pereira's initial Modernist design consisted of three separate pavilions with slender colonnades supporting the overhanging roofs. The marble and glass pavilions were positioned around a U-shaped courtyard that opened toward Wilshire Boulevard. The museum campus sat on a raised plaza above a shimmering pool of water with fountains. The LACMA complex was surrounded by landscaping and, taking advantage of the region's mild climate, incorporated outdoor areas into the function of the museum. This plan literally and conceptually elevated the museum above daily life, while at the same time keeping it open to the city around it.

In the original proposal, the Ahmanson pavilion was to house most of the museum's permanent art collection, the Bart Lytton pavilion was to present traveling exhibitions and the Bing pavilion was to contain an auditorium, an educational facility, a library and a dining area. Ground was broken on November 8, 1962, and the museum officially opened on March 31, 1964. The Lytton pavilion was renamed after Armand Hammer in 1969. Despite official praise, the museum design was not seen as particularly hospitable to the display of art. Shortly after it opened, the reflecting pools around the museum were filled in, in part because tar began to seep into the water. In the late 1960s and early 1970s, museum trustees, planning for the museum's expansion, began discussing the acquisition of May Company's appliance building and parking structure located to the west, and of the Prudential property located to the east. Some of the plans eventually came through— the May Company property is currently part of LACMA.

In the mid-1980s, the museum campus went through a major spatial redesign. The architecture firm of Hardy, Holzman, Pfeiffer Associates designed the 115,000-square-foot Anderson Building to display modern and contemporary art. That building, which in 2007 was renamed the Art of the Americas Building, opened in November 1986. Visually, this addition squared off the original U-shaped plan of the complex. In the process of enclosing the museum from Wilshire Boulevard, the architects designed an enormous asymmetrical front facing Wilshire. This structure, compared at the time to a postmodern Babylonian wall, was composed of tawny colored Minnesota limestone set with bluish green glass blocks and laced throughout with bands of green terra cotta. The wall framed the main entrance that led up a stairwell bordered by a channel of water running along its east side into a pool in the sculpture garden. Seventy-foot-high columns, clad in deep

green terra cotta, supported a translucent canopy that filtered natural light into the courtyard. In 1988, a new pavilion for Japanese Art opened, initially designed by Bruce Goff and finished by his associate Bart Prince. In 1994, LACMA acquired the May Company properties, adjacent to the west, and renamed the May Company building LACMA West.

In 2001, the museum's board of trustees approved a plan to transform the museum campus. Five internationally known architects were invited to present proposals: Jean Nouvel, Thom Mayne, Steven Holl, Daniel Libeskind and Rem Koolhaas. The competition narrowed to two architects, Nouvel and Koolhaas, and eventually the Koolhaas plan, which proposed to raze all of the museum's six buildings and replace them with a single tent-like megastructure, was selected. Philosophically, it affirmed Los Angeles's reputation as a city unbound by the conventional traditions of the original museum plan. Nevertheless, and partly because of the unsuccessful drive to raise funds for its $300 million price tag, the Koolhaas plan was not built.

In 2003, the architect Renzo Piano was asked to create a new master plan. The Piano plan called for two new buildings and for resituating the museum's entry at Ogden Drive, to the west of the old entrance. To link the disparate parts of LACMA, including the May Company building, an eight-hundred-foot-long pedestrian spine would cut across the entire site. Piano's six-thousand-square-foot Broad Contemporary Art Museum, a travertine-clad, three-story pavilion, opened in 2008. Entry to the building is on the third floor, reachable via an exterior escalator and stairwells, which also include platforms at various levels with views toward Hollywood Hills. Piano's one-story Resnick Pavilion, also clad in travertine and bordered by a landscape designed by the artist Robert Irwin, opened in 2010. In accordance with Piano's plans, the current entrance to the LACMA campus is on Ogden Drive, through the now iconic forest-like sculptural installation of old streetlights by Chris Burden called *Urban Lights*.

LACMA is the largest, but not the only, cultural institution in this location. In 1913, George Allan Hancock granted the newly founded Los Angeles County Museum of History, Science and Art exclusive right for scientific digs on his property. Hancock also offered to donate the twenty-three acres

Opposite, top: This aerial view from 1968 shows the U-shaped plan around which the original three LACMA pavilions were built. *Courtesy of "Dick" Whittington.*

Opposite, bottom: Partial view of the LACMA courtyard redesigned by Hardy, Holzman, Pfeiffer Associates in the late 1980s. Photographed in 2010. *Courtesy of Ruth Wallach.*

to the County of Los Angeles, a gift that was finalized in 1924, after which the property became known as Hancock Park. The park, designated as a national Natural Landmark in 1964, is considered to be one of the world's richest Pleistocene fossil sites. Digs are ongoing and may be viewed by tourists strolling through the park.

In 1973, millionaire George C. Page, a trustee of the Los Angeles County Natural History Museum Foundation, offered Los Angeles County a $2.5 million gift to finance the building of a museum that would house the fossils found in the La Brea Tar Pits. The George C. Page Museum at the La Brea Tar Pits, designed by Thornton, Fagan and Associates, is structured around a landscaped central atrium. Manuel Paz designed the elaborate frieze that wraps around the upper façade of the museum. It depicts a landscape and animals that populated this area during the Pleistocene period. The museum opened in April 1977. That year, to celebrate the fiftieth anniversary of Hancock Park, it loaned to the Ohrbach's department store, which was by then located on the southeast corner of Wilshire and Fairfax, several fossil skeletons. The store exhibited the fossils as part of its window display of new fashion.

When in the 1910s George Allan Hancock proposed to give the land to the County of Los Angeles so that it would become a scientific park open to

This sculpture of fighting saber-toothed cats, designed by Herman T. Beck in 1934, is located in Hancock Park. In the background is a detail of the frieze by Manuel Paz that wraps around the exterior of the Page Museum. Photographed in 2012. *Courtesy of Ruth Wallach.*

the public, he included several improvement clauses, one of which stipulated the placement of life-size sculptural replicas to represent specific animals. Several sculptural groups depicting prehistoric animals were designed for Hancock Park, and most of them are still here. Three life-size saber-toothed cats fighting over the carcass of a bison were executed by Herman T. Beck from a design by Joseph L. Roop in 1934. Beck also produced a group of two lions in 1935, a bear sitting on a boulder in 1936 and two ground sloths in 1938. These cement sculptures were financed through the Works Progress Administration (WPA).

In 1951, as the park was undergoing relandscaping, the sculptures were moved to the area around the lake pit, next to Wilshire Boulevard, where one of the saber-toothed tigers and the carcass of the bison disappeared. The remaining sculptures are currently located at various places in the park. In the mid-1960s, the museum board awarded the sculptor Howard Ball a grant to sculpt additional statues for Hancock Park. Ball's sculptural group made of fiberglass included the still extant mammoth family positioned around the lake. Ball executed several other sculptures for the park, some of which were stolen or vandalized. The park is also home to a bronze bust of George Allan Hancock by Holger and Helen Jensen.

6067 Wilshire Boulevard, Northeast Corner with Fairfax Avenue

May Company opened its five-story Wilshire store, dubbed the "Store of Tomorrow," in early September 1939 on a lot that once held a horse stable and was later the site of various automobile shows. The cost of construction, fixtures, etc., was a reported $2 million. The building's design took advantage of its location on a major intersection, with both the Fairfax and Wilshire façades given equal visual importance. May Company's first-floor display windows were lined with black granite, and the famous corner tower, purportedly modeled after a perfume bottle, was clad in gold-colored Italian glass mosaic. In the interior, the lobby was decorated in lime yellow and dusty pink colors. For a while, the mezzanine had a circulating library, and there was a roof-garden restaurant. Despite its impressive street façade, the store's major entrance was oriented toward the parking lot, which was built to hold six hundred cars. The lot was located north of the store and included a full-service automotive station.

Albert C. Martin designed the Streamline Moderne–style May Company building, and Samuel A. Marx designed the interior furnishings and

The first floor of the May Company store photographed on opening day, September 9, 1939. *Courtesy of the* Examiner.

decorations. In 1940, the company purchased the entire block immediately to the east, which was owned by the University of Southern California. The original impetus for the expansion was to construct a "modern television and frequency modulation transmission station and studio"; it later became known as the May Company Wilshire Appliance Building. In 1953, the company constructed a three-level parking garage to accommodate over one thousand cars behind the appliance building. The May Company Building, which is currently part of the LACMA campus, was designated Los Angeles Historic Cultural Monument #566 on September 30, 1992.

6101 Wilshire Boulevard, Northwest Corner with Fairfax Avenue

In 1924, this corner was the location of the tract office of the Evans Ferguson Corporation, among the developers affiliated with A.W. Ross. Rogers airfield and the oil fields operated by the Gilmore Company were also located nearby. Beginning with the 1930s, this corner had various drive-in eateries. A building designed by Louis Armet and Eldon Davis in 1955 as Romeo's Time Square restaurant is still located here. Its Space Age, or Googie, design featured a large neon sign on the restaurant's roof. Smooth and sleek in its geometry, its purpose was to grab the attention of drivers and beckon them inside. As Cynthia Daniels wrote in her 2004 *Los Angeles Times* article "Googie Fans Have Goo-Goo Eyes for L.A. Coffee Shop":

> *Glass windows encased the building, allowing passersby to see inside. The kitchen was in plain view so customers could watch their food being cooked. Leather counter seats appeared suspended in air, thanks to a cantilevered design. A mural of Manhattan's Times Square and New York City occupied the west wall.*

Romeo's stayed here until the early 1960s, when it became Ram's eatery. Later that decade, it was renamed Johnie's, which closed in 2003. The building and its iconic sign are occasionally used for filming. Johnie's parking lot is currently used to service the 99-Cent store immediately to the west, located on the site of the Royal Food Center store.

View of Johnie's Coffee Shop, designed by Armet and Davis in 1955. Photographed in 2013. *Courtesy of Ruth Wallach.*

Hauser Boulevard to Fairfax Avenue, South Side

5650-5680 Wilshire Boulevard,
Entire Block between Hauser Boulevard and Masselin Avenue

This lot on the south side of Wilshire Boulevard just west of Hauser was developed as a commercial structure that by 1932 housed Citizens National Bank and other businesses. In 1948, Citizens National Bank moved a few blocks west to the southeast corner of Wilshire Boulevard and Curson Avenue. A new building was constructed for California Federal Bank, which moved to this block facing Masselin that same year. Although the structure was expanded in the 1950s, California Federal, which grew considerably, planned a new headquarters in this location.

The current complex, a plaza with a twenty-eight-story office tower rising in the center, was designed by Charles Luckman Associates and cost $17 million. In June 1958, several dignitaries rode to the groundbreaking ceremony in an ox cart to commemorate this location as a former wheat field on Rancho Las Cienegas. The contract for the structure was awarded to Vinnell and Haas and Hynie Corporation, which constructed some of the other post–World War II buildings on Miracle Mile. When the high rise was completed in late 1964, it was considered to be among the tallest commercial skyscrapers in Southern California. It had an auditorium on the third floor that could accommodate 250 people. Fountains and a lagoon with a bridge leading to the Wilshire entry were planned, as well as a heliport, the latter typical of Los Angeles skyscrapers. True to the car culture of mid-century Los Angeles, the complex had accommodations for over two thousand automobiles.

California Federal promoted its investment into the tower as a fundamental expression of its confidence in the economic well-being of Miracle Mile. The diamond-shaped building opened on February 15, 1965, and in March of that year, the Crocker-Citizens' National Bank, successor to the Citizens Bank that originally occupied this location, moved one of its branches into a commercial space in the plaza. Like many Modernist commercial structures, the design of the California Federal building was sculptural, with the column-like tower sitting on a wide base. Its main Wilshire lobby was decorated in gold, beige, brown, burnt orange and yellow hues, with a finish of Montezuma travertine from Arizona and terrazzo floor tiles. The walls were decorated with two large

Above: This California Federal Bank building, photographed in 1952, was located on the southeast corner of Wilshire Boulevard and Masselin Avenue from 1948 until about 1963. *Courtesy of the* Examiner.

Right: This diamond-shaped office tower, designed for California Federal by Charles Luckman in 1963–64, has housed several financial institutions over the years. Photographed in 2012. *Courtesy of Ruth Wallach.*

tapestries, one by the French designer Lucret and the other by the American muralists Arthur and Jean Ames. *Structure and Flow*, a large fountain designed by Claire Falkenstein, was located west of the main entrance. It was a swirling tangle of copper pipes and Venetian glass, approximately forty-five by thirty feet, standing seventeen feet above a pool, with welded copper tubes gushing water. According to the artist, the fountain was a sculptural piece made out of water that created light effects through reflections of copper and glass. As a piece of abstract sculpture, the fountain almost immediately became an object of both admiration and derision. In January 1970, California Federal hosted an exhibition of sculpture, painting and ceramics by Claire Falkenstein in the foyer of the auditorium and several illustrated lectures by the artist. When the building was undergoing major remodeling in 1990, the fountain was supposedly dismantled by the artist and moved to storage. Its whereabouts are unknown, and it may have been melted down.

5700-5780 Wilshire Boulevard. Entire Block between Masselin and Curson Avenues

In 1948, Citizens National Trust & Savings Bank opened its branch on the southeast corner with Curson Avenue. Its two-story Modernist building was designed by Stiles O. Clements. The structure was of reinforced concrete and partly faced with Arizona flagstone. The interior décor was of green and yellow hues, with Honduras mahogany finish, said to be an example of California Modern design. Citizens Bank moved to this location from the southwest corner of Wilshire and Hauser Boulevards, which it occupied since 1932. East of it was located the furniture store Harry Gladstone, occupying 5760 Wilshire since the 1940s. In 1962, Donavan and Seamans, a venerable Los Angeles jewelry store, replaced Harry Gladstone, moving from its previous address west of Hauser Boulevard, at which point the façade was redecorated by Eugene Burke, Charles M. Kober and Harold J. Nicolais. It was faced with green Italian marble and featured a bronze clock. The black sidewalk in front of the building provided a striking contrast to the store's white marble entry.

The Wilshire Courtyard complex, currently occupying the entire block, opened in 1987, replacing the low-rise commercial buildings. The Courtyard is an office and retail complex of one million square feet, developed in partnership between J.H. Snyder Company, Museum Square Associates and California Federal Savings. Designed by McLarand, Vasquez & Partners, Inc., and costing approximately $185 million, it is composed of two six-story geometric wave-shaped buildings clad in red granite that face each other over a large courtyard. Pyramidal skylights add an Art Deco flavor to the otherwise unadorned façades. At the time it was built, given its massive scale, Wilshire Courtyard was criticized for not reflecting the rich early twentieth-century architectural heritage of Miracle Mile. Fong & Associates designed a landscaping plan not just for greenery but also to include a quarter-mile jogging track. Plantings of coral trees alternating with Washingtonia and Queen palm trees framed the main courtyard, noted for its fountains and slate-clad sculptural obelisks.

In order to accommodate the wishes of the neighboring residential community, a two-acre strip of land was developed as park to act as a buffer between the offices and the single-family residences located south of Eighth Street. It was rededicated in 2008 as Wilshire Green Park. During the rededication, a bronze sculpture by Corrine Weinberg was placed in the center of the park at the end of Courtyard Place. Wilshire Green Park features a pond with live turtles, a children's playground and several curving graveled walkways. Wilshire Courtyard was part of J.H. Snyder Company's effort to bring new life

The building for Citizens Bank, photographed in 1948, was designed by Stiles O. Clements for the southeast corner of Wilshire Boulevard and Curson Avenue. *Courtesy of the* Examiner.

Wilshire Courtyard, constructed in 1987, spans several blocks between Masselin and Curson Avenues. The tower built for California Federal Bank is seen in the background. Photographed in 2012. *Courtesy of Ruth Wallach*.

Wilshire Green Park, photographed in 2012, is a buffer between the Wilshire Courtyard complex and the single-family residential areas to its south. *Courtesy of Ruth Wallach*.

View of the bronze sculpture by Corrine Weinberg, located in the center of Wilshire Green Park. Photographed in 2012. *Courtesy of Ruth Wallach.*

to the then declining Miracle Mile. Jerry Snyder, an Orange County–based builder who also bought and renovated the 1948 Prudential Building on the north side of Wilshire Boulevard, planned to add residential units within the Courtyard complex. This did not come to fruition.

5800-5820 Wilshire Boulevard.
Entire Block between Curson and Stanley Avenues

The two-story building on the southwest corner with Curson Avenue was constructed in 1958 for Prudential Insurance Company by the Donald R. Warren Company on what was a vacant lot. The structure was built on a floating foundation that could support additional floors. The circa 1930 building to the west, at 5814 Wilshire, housed The Egg and The Eye, a

Above: This 2012 photograph shows the southwest corner of Wilshire Boulevard and Curson Avenue, including the Craft and Folk Art Museum and the six-story building to the west of it, designed by McDonald and Parsons. *Courtesy of Ruth Wallach.*

Left: Stiles O. Clements designed the Arthur Murray Dance studio in 1942. It is seen in the right foreground of this 1948 photograph. The Prudential Building is in the background to the left. *Courtesy of "Dick" Whittington.*

restaurant and art gallery specializing in craft and folk art that was co-founded in 1966 by Edith Wyle and Bette Chase. In 1976, the gallery earned nonprofit status and became the Craft and Folk Art Museum (CAFAM). A street sign commemorating Edith Wyle was recently installed nearby. CAFAM closed in the late 1980s and reopened in 1995 in renovated quarters, which were enlarged by Hodgetts+Fung Design Associates.

At 5820 Wilshire is a Modernist six-story steel frame commercial building with concrete slab floors and reinforced brick masonry. It was designed in 1959 by Jack H. McDonald and Cejay Parsons, who also designed the large sign structure on the roof. The building's Wilshire Boulevard façade is a curtain wall of aluminum mullions, glass and porcelain-on-aluminum panels.

In 1942, Stiles O. Clements designed a building for the Arthur Murray Dance studio at 5828 Wilshire Boulevard on the southeast corner with Stanley Avenue. The design included a tall sign-bearing tower, which eventually was incorporated into the McDonald and Parsons building immediately to the east. The interior of the Murray Building was paneled in California redwood. In the late 1960s, the radio station KLAC had offices in this building. Stiles O. Clements and Associates also designed the building at 5850–5858 Wilshire, on the southwest corner with Stanley, for the Veterans Aircraft & Automotive Insurance Company. The Modernist exterior of this 1951 building is clad in Roman brick.

5900 Wilshire Boulevard.
Entire Block between Spaulding Avenue and Ogden Drive

For several decades after the 1936–37 "California House and Garden Exhibition" described in chapter three, Ross and his partners planned to develop this block into what they called Theater Square, with various plans drawn up to include such cultural facilities as an opera house, a theater, artists' studios, galleries and apartments. In the early 1960s, Ross began planning for a two-tower apartment complex designed by Irving D. Shapiro. Although none of these early plans were realized, they were part of Ross's vision for Miracle Mile as a dense commercial and residential corridor, where all amenities would be located within walking distance. By the 1970s, the mid-Wilshire area had become home to advertising and insurance companies.

In 1969, a thirty-two-story office tower, designed by William L. Pereira Associates for a joint venture between Mutual Benefit Life Insurance Company (developers of Parklabrea) and Walter H. Shorenstein, a San Francisco–based developer, was constructed. Pereira's original 1965 proposal was for two twenty-four-story office buildings, with exterior columns spaced to mirror his design for the Los Angeles County Museum of Art, which opened a year earlier on the opposite side of Wilshire Boulevard. The final design, constructed in 1969 by Haas and Haynie Corporation, cost $20 million and consisted of a central tower flanked by two two-story buildings, all rising from a plaza landscaped with fountains and reflecting pools. It was said to be the largest structure and among the tallest on the entire Wilshire

The Variety Tower at 5900 Wilshire Boulevard, photographed looking southeast in 2013. *Courtesy of Ruth Wallach.*

Boulevard at that time. A subterranean parking facility for eight hundred cars was also built. From 1994 to 2000, the Carole Kaye and Barry Kaye Museum of Miniatures was located here. In 2006, the A+D Architecture and Design Museum moved to this location for a few years. In November 2009, the Wende Museum, a cultural institution with the mission to preserve Cold War artifacts and history, commemorated the twentieth anniversary of the dismantling of the Berlin Wall by installing segments of the original wall in front of the building. The Wende commissioned the artists Thierry Noir, Kent Twitchell, Farrah Karapetian and Marie Astrid González to paint some of the segments.

6000 Wilshire Boulevard.
Entire Block between Ogden Drive and Orange Grove Avenue

In the late 1950s, various Modernist commercial buildings were planned for the corner lot, notably by Welton Becket (1957) and Sidney Eisenshtat (1959),

The medical building designed by Sidney Eisenshtat in 1953 (left) and the two-story building designed by Milton J. Black in 1936 are seen in this 2013 photograph. *Courtesy of Ruth Wallach.*

although it remains a parking lot to this day. The five-story structure located at 6010 Wilshire was designed by Sidney Eisenshtat in 1953 as a medical building. Its façade is finished in gunmetal-colored porcelain, hung from steel trusses. Horizontal bands of glass run along the width of the building. Its drive-in entrance was designed to unload patients directly to the main lobby. The two-story commercial building immediately to the west was designed in 1936 by Milton J. Black. The rest of the building block was finished in the late 1930s and early 1940s. Currently, it is occupied by architecture-related cultural institutions. A+D Architecture and Design Museum, which relocated into 6032 Wilshire in 2010, occupies an interior space that was redesigned by the architecture firms Richard Meier & Partners and Gensler.

6060 Wilshire Boulevard,
Entire Block between Orange Grove and Fairfax Avenues

The Ben Bard Playhouse and School, established in 1920, was located on the southwest side of Orange Grove Avenue, behind a gasoline station. Eventually, it changed its name to Max Reinhardt Theatre Workshop and then to Geller Theatre Workshop. In the 1950s, it became known as Theatre of Arts and stayed in this location until circa 1960. Seibu Corporation, a Japanese department store, bought the entire block in 1959 for more than $6 million, in what turned out to be an unsuccessful attempt to enter the Los Angeles retail market. The building for the Seibu store was designed by Welton Becket and Associates in collaboration with a Tokyo-based landscape architectural firm. The initial design, notable for eight sixty-foot-tall columns that were to rise from four large reflecting pools along the Wilshire Boulevard frontage, blended contemporary American architectural design with Japanese forms. When it was built, vermilion-colored Japanese glass mosaic tile decorated the exterior of the store along the second floor and contrasted with a band of specially designed shoji screen-like windows on the third floor. Cylindrical frosted glass lanterns suspended from the roof overhang illuminated the front entrance on Wilshire Boulevard. The entrances on Wilshire and Fairfax were framed by vaulted canopies, in imitation of the overhanging eaves prevalent in traditional Japanese architecture.

The *Los Angeles Times* proclaimed that the store would change Americans' long-held impression that goods from East Asia were cheap imitations of Western designs. Thousands of people came on opening day, March 15, 1962, and watched as a cherry tree was planted with great ceremony on the Fairfax Avenue side. The upscale store proved unprofitable and closed in March 1964, with the company announcing that the building would become a Japanese industrial exhibition center. It stood vacant for several years, although Island in the Sky, a glass-enclosed Japanese restaurant, located on the fourth (penthouse) floor, remained open until August 1967. That year,

Petersen's Automotive Museum is located in a building originally designed by Welton Becket in 1962 for Seibu department store. Photographed in 2012. *Courtesy of Ruth Wallach.*

Los Angeles County supervisors attempted to acquire the Seibu building for a new paleontology museum to be operated by the County Museum of Natural History. That project fell through for lack of funding. Ohrbach's department store bought the building in late 1967, planning to add close to sixty-eight thousand square feet to the south. The interior of the store was redesigned by Paul Laszlo and Chaix & Johnson Associates. Ohrbach's closed its previous location in the Prudential Building and opened the new store in August 1969. In the 1980s, Ohrbach's was among the many retail chain stores hit hard by changes in customer tastes and by the success of discount clothing stores and closed this location in December 1986.

Petersen's Automotive Museum, the building's current occupant, was named for its benefactors Margie and Robert E. Petersen, the latter founder and chairman of Petersen Publishing Co., publisher of various car-related magazines. In 1994, the Petersens donated $15 million to the Los Angeles County Natural History Museum to start a museum devoted to automobile history and culture. The Natural History Museum, which began collecting automobiles in the 1930s, also received $20 million in bond money from the county for the new museum. In 2000, the Petersens contributed over $24 million to retire the bond debt and to establish the Petersen Automotive Museum Foundation as an independent nonprofit organization to operate the museum. The Wilshire Boulevard façade was redesigned in 1994 by Mark Whipple of the Russell Group to evoke the radiator grill of a car. In the late 1990s, a monster truck protruded from the top floor of the building on the Fairfax Avenue side.

6100 Wilshire Boulevard, Southwest Corner with Fairfax Avenue

Developer William S. Rosecrans purchased this lot, which had a gasoline station, in 1938. Various plans to develop this corner, including one by Stiles O. Clements for a Bond's Clothing store, did not materialize. A Thrifty Drugstore building, designed by Clements, opened here in 1951 to great fanfare. The company advertised this store as an example of modern functional design. As Miracle Mile went into economic decline, Thrifty's was demolished. The New Wilshire, a slender sixteen-story glass and stainless steel tower, was built on this corner in 1985 and still stands at this location. The $45 million building was designed by William L. Pereira Associates for the developer Mahoney-Sewell Associates and was hailed as the first major new structure in the Miracle Mile area in more than a decade. The building was considered a lynchpin in the district's economic revitalization

Thrifty Drugstore, designed by Stiles O. Clements, is shown here shortly after it opened in 1951 on the southwest corner of Wilshire and Fairfax. *Courtesy of the* Examiner.

New Wilshire was designed by William Pereira in 1985 for the southwest corner of Wilshire and Fairfax. Photographed in 2012. *Courtesy of Ruth Wallach.*

and was called the Miracle on Miracle Mile by the *Los Angeles Times*. William Pereira designed it so that the windows would open onto small stainless-steel balconies that provided not only views but also fresh air. A five-story underground garage was part of the design. The landscape was originally designed by Robert Herrick Carter and Associates.

At a time when large corporations were leaving the Miracle Mile area, Mahoney-Sewell Associates advertised the property to businesses with fewer than fifty employees. Such businesses, according to the company, employed more than 80 percent of the Los Angeles workforce. This was the same strategy the company implemented earlier at its Two Transamerica Center in San Francisco, also designed by Pereira. In a manner similar to Alvah Warren Ross's publicity for Miracle Mile in the 1920s, New Wilshire was hailed as being within easy access to downtown Los Angeles, Westwood and Beverly Hills.

SELECTED BIBLIOGRAPHY

Banham, Reyner. *Los Angeles: The Architecture of Four Ecologies*. New York: Penguin Books, 1971.

Clover, Samuel Travers. *A Pioneer Heritage*. Los Angeles: Saturday Night Publishing Company, 1932.

De Wit, Wim, and Christopher James Alexander. *Overdrive: L.A. Constructs the Future, 1940–1990*. Los Angeles: Getty Research Institute, 2013.

"Exhibition House Group, Los Angeles, California." *Architectural Forum* 65 (July 1936): 37–46.

Hancock, Ralph. *Fabulous Boulevard*. New York: Funk & Wagnall Co, 1949.

Hunt, William Dudley. *Total Design; Architecture of Welton Becket and Associates*. New York: McGraw-Hill, 1971.

Kimball, Bernice. *Street Names of Los Angeles*. Los Angeles: Bureau of Engineering, 1988.

Longstreth, Richard W. *City Center to Regional Mall: Architecture, the Automobile, and Retailing in Los Angeles, 1920–1950*. Cambridge, MA: MIT Press, 1997.

Smith, Laura Massino. *Architecture Tours, L.A. Guidebook: Hancock Park/Miracle Mile*. Atglen, PA: Schiffer Pub., 2005.

Weiss, Marc A. *The Rise of the Community Builders: The American Real Estate Industry and Urban Land Planning*. New York: Columbia University Press, 1987.

William L. Pereira Associates. *The Wilshire Central Concept*. Los Angeles: W.L. Pereira Associates, 1970.

ABOUT THE AUTHOR

R uth Wallach is the head of the Helen Topping Architecture and Fine Arts Library at the University of Southern California. She has previously coauthored several historic photography books about Los Angeles.